Yakub And The Origins of White Supremacy

Message to the Whiteman & Woman in America

By
Dorothy Blake Farda

Lushena Books, Inc.

Message to the Whiteman & Woman in America

Dorothy Blake Fardan

Printed September, 2001

Published and Distributed By:
Lushena Books, Inc.
607 Country Club Drive Unit E
Bensonville, IL 60106

ISBN: 1-930097-28-X

Printed in the United States of America

DEDICATED TO

My husband, Brother D., who introduced me to Islam, the teachings of the Honorable Elijah Muhammad, and the world of Africans here in the wilderness of North America,

AND

with gratitude and love for my parents, and those Africans who helped to shape and form my childhood world in rural Kentucky.

ACKNOWLEDGEMENTS

I would like to extend my gratitude towards those students through the years whose questions, opposition, and sometimes agreement, often inspired me to dig deepr for answers and to continue on in the effort to arrive at the truth.

Special Gratitude is owed to The Staff of United Brothers & Sisters Communications Systems, my publishers, for their generous response of time and consideration in reading the manuscript, their support for its worth, and the decision to publish.

And affection is expressed to Mary Francis Slaughter for her material support in the first stages of the book.

CONTENTS

PREFACE-1996

(Third printing, 1996)

In the five years since publication, I have become even more convinced that the message to the *White Man and Woman in America* must be delivered. I am also firmly assured, now, as I was then, that there is a message to Caucasian People within the Message to the Blackman in America, as put forth by the Honorable Elijah Muhammad.

Much has taken place in the last five years; historically relevant events have occurred which have impacted the question of "race" in America, and indeed globally. For this reason I feel the book is even more timely and should be useful in any discussion of race or racism.

But I have also learned that media, in the form of talk shows as well as news, is not really interested in discussing racism, which is white supremacy. At best it will only discuss it in the context of examining-white separatist and neo-nazi groups as fringe and extremist populations. This allows the rest of white America to feel comfortably distanced and uninvolved in anything considered to be white supremacy. Any serious analysis of the rule of white supremacy as a socio-economic political order that governs the entire collective psyche and cultural institutions here in the United States and elsewhere in the world, is therefore avoided and nullified by media agendas.

It is sad, indeed tragic, that following the O.J. Simpson- trial talk shows rushed to discuss "race relations" by parading interracial couples, their friends, enemies, relatives, and associates before already programmed audiences, to argue and debate over-personal attitudes and relationships, interracial dating and marriage, and bi-racial children.

The "real deal" (that is, the system of white supremacy that governs every institutional sector of the society--education, religion, the courts, prisons, health care, politics, etc.) remains unchallenged in public discourse.

Consequently, any day of the week television viewers can

turn on a variety of talk shows which feature some black man sitting between several women, usually white, sometimes white and black, being questioned by a white talk show host and her/his selected and primed studio audience, about the man's multiple love affairs and irresponsible fatherings. The stereotypes jump out blatantly. Somewhere in the scenario a white expect (psychiatrist, marriage counselor, therapist is brought out to counsel the men and women about proper relations and marriage. Some of these guests who would have no other venue for coming before a group of people like this, give their best shot at entertaining and provoking the already hyped-up audience. They rap and confront their angry mates, frequently drawing huge amounts of laughter or outrage from the viewers. It amounts to the same old buffoonery that has mesmerized white America for centuries.

Young white women, called "wanna be's" by their families and friends, are questioned about why they like black men and black life, but are never queried about their views on white America and what seems to be missing from their white lives. When they do try to articulate some reasons, they are shouted down as being rebellious, racist and irresponsible. Older white people are interrogated on being prejudiced and behind times, but seldom if ever do talk shows focused on the historical evolution of the societal order (the system of white supremacy) and its being established on the plunder and exploitation of people of color. Those few shows which do try to incorporate some kind of historical critique, end up blocking the impact of accurate historical information by "balancing" the show, with guests whom they know will introduce argument and confusion so that the audience never hears a continuous flow of explanation and documentation that would clarify; he issues. Therefore, most people in America and elsewhere still do not understand their involvement in and perpetuation of white supremacy.

All people but most especially white Americans, need to mow actual facts and the truth of history .That is why the section on "White supremacy and the rejection of history" in chapter One is so essential. I would repeat a million times ver if I could the words on page 13: "This ignorance, and section of history allows whites to continue in illusions of greatness and white supremacy that can only be eliminated *y* unfolding the layers of rejected history ." And "in rejecting le truth of Black history (all the way back to beginnings" they have rejected the truth of themselves and the crucial key to unlocking the doors to both the past and present, and therefore, any clear oath towards the future."

As far as changing any parts of the book, I wouldn't. But there are places that could use some clarification. For ample, some readers have mis-interpreted the section on "Grafting" (page 132), when I discuss a genetic perspective eliminating white supremacy. I say: "But, from a perfectly logical perspective, a Caucasian who might take IS grafting solution seriously and from a perspective that IV grafting as a way to return to an original nature, intermarriage would constitute the long range process of grafting back into the original, and thus would be desirable." In other words, the dominant genes (associated with darkness or blackness) would prevail, and recessive genes (whiteness) would be absorbed, eventually being overwhelmed by the original. This would, simply on the is of logic, end the possibility of white supremacy. I go of course to explain the differing views on such "mixing;" some see this as diluting and weakening the Original or Black people; and others who are truly white supremacist would fear any mixing and the possibility of genetic annihilation.

Some interpreted this as a call for intermarriage or integration. Integration is a term that has very little to do with personal love affairs and marriage choices. Rather, it relates more to the concept of colonization and describes what happens to an oppressed people (in this case African or Black People in America) when they accept their oppressor's (the European or white people's) terms for participation in the oppressor's social system. While many Black people and whites alike might have believed for years that integration was " opening doors," "forging new levels of equality," and generating "equal opportunity," the reality is that integration only furthered the Parasitic relationship between whites and Blacks, making Black people more dependent on white institutions while their own few independent institutions such as small businesses, schools and churches, began to falter because of social and economic anemia--that is, all the rich nutrients of Black labor and dollars were still feeding the blood-sucking whites who owned the means of production and the banks that stored all the wealth.

Integration translates into domestic or internal colonialism

Black communities are colonies under white supremacist rule in the United States and allover the world. Certainly I did not call for this! Whites who happen to be involved in "mixed" marriages need to identify with the Black Liberation struggle and the liberation struggle of all oppressed peoples, and they need to reject the integrationist mind set which will only extend their loved ones further into oppression, dependency, and self-denial. The white "mate" has to let go of white America and quit talking about teaching their children "both of the cultures" they descend from, as if there is something their children should want to identify with in white history and culture. There isn't! They need to be taught the straight-up truth about white history and what the European ancestors and predecessors did, and if there were any who struggled against the power structure of white supremacy, like John Brown, or created beauty in spite of white supremacy, like some of the musicians and artists, then tell them that. But there is nothing worth hanging on to in "white or European history." It is a history and culture of death.

So, this section of the book has been misunderstood and I suspect will, always be troublesome. But I'll let it stand.

I probably would add new names to the section where I talk about Caucasian men and women who do not seem to resent white supremacy in behavior or sentiment. These are people who have escaped or overcome the attributes of white supremacy. "There are women like Ida Hakim (Founder of C.U.R.E.) along with Ferrell Winfree and Betty Shafer whom I did not know at the time I wrote the book, and whom today I regard as sisters in the struggle to combat racism and the rule of white supremacy as well as to establish justice and secure reparations for African descendants of slaves and native Indigenous peoples. Len Moritz also has joined in this effort. And there is Seifullah Ali Shabazz up in Passiac, New Jersey --a strong Caucasian Muslim brother who has struggled in the cause of truth for a number of years.

Still others I don't know personally, like Father Fleger of St. Sabina's in Chicago, and Todd Leech, BCAC, Milwaukee, both community activists who defy the requisites of male white supremacy thought and ,behavior . And there are others, both men and women, who do good deeds in spite of the racist social system they may not have yet brought into question. I would hope the names of

Caucasians resisting and combating white supremacy would increase and circulate through the next few years. Certainly these sections of the book were not intended to be exclusive nor exhaustive.

I am sure there would be books to add to the list at the end of the book, as well as other publications. And I would encourage listening to and supporting public Broadcasting, stations or Black-owned ones few though they may be. I failed to mention radio station WOL, (Black owned) and WDCU (public) in the 'Washington, D.C. area where I am located. These are alternative sources for getting information that counters the white-out in mainstream media. I mentioned the "For the People" series (South Carolina Educational T.V.), but recently the great interviewer and host, Listervelt Middleton, passed away. The series will be a legacy I am sure which will be passed on to generations who have not yet seem them.

This book was not intended to a lengthy, in-depth research project. It was intended to deliver a message, with enough evidence hopefully to stimulate readers to seek further information and do their own research. There are parts which could have involved more time and deeper research. Rather than rewrite the book, I have done more extensive and comprehensive research for the next book, forthcoming, entitled The Last Exodus: The End of White Suuremacy and the Return of the Original.

Lastly, the momentous Million Man March took place during the five years since this publication. Minister Louis Farrakhan's profound speech and his 1996 Savior's Day Address have confirmed in my heart that the Nation of Islam under the guidance and founding by Master Fard Muhammad and the Ron. Elijah Muhammad has provided the wisdom and light for human salvation not just for the Lost-Found Original (Black) people in the Wilderness of North America, but the human family in general. The Nation's message which has been maligned and vilified through the years as "reverse racism" and "'hate-filled rhetoric" in actuality is a message of both painful truth and universal healing. Under its canopy of 360 degrees Truth and directives for self-knowing and self-mastery, all peoples can gain knowledge of themselves, the world they live in and guidance for attaining personal and collective justice.

This kind of Islam does not lay in the past, but it lies in the human heart that submits to the Originator of its pulsing life. When the heart rallies to the rule of righteousness and peace, the *rule* of white supremacy can no longer exist nor exert power over the human family.

Dorothy Blake Fardan
Spring, 1996

INTRODUCTION

In 1970, I encountered a strange new kind of thinking in the teachings of the Honorable Elijah Muhammad. It was the way one of his students presented them to me. I recall the feeling I had when I listened to this person speak on subjects like "Original Man," "Yakub's History" "The Last Days" and the "Mother Ship." It was a feeling of falling into some deep and fathomless pool of knowledge that somehow could heal the mental and emotional lesions that Western thought had left me with. For some time, I had experienced an imprisoned sensation when it came to knowledge; all that I had read and learned in my years of IIschooling'I seemed to be insufficient, inadequate, and dead. For years I had read all that Western philosophy had to offer; studied its theology, raced through psychology and sociology, and still felt lost, locked up, empty, with no place to go.

MESSAGE TO THE BLACKMAN IN AMERICA (by the Honorable Elijah Muhammad) was a message to me, a Caucasian woman. It opened up the long lost tunnel of origins that I had failed to penetrate in all my efforts to see the past. It confirmed my estrangement from America, and it sketched out a future in which I could hope to carve out some place within, despite my less than noble white legacy. That others thought my attachment to these teachings a bit abnormal if not insane, didn't really bother me, because I felt the nearness of truth in them, and for once in my then thirty years sojourn on this earth, I felt someone had reached into some absolute bottom that lay beneath the facade and fantasy of the white world I was struggling to get out of.

I understood that it was Islam that had formed the womb of Elijah Muhammad's liberation, and that unlocked my own mental incarceration, and I would never forget that. I also understood that it was racist white America that provided the background and stage out of which this messenger would deliver the principles of Islam. I could never embrace the truth of one without being aware of the other.

Somehow as I incorporated Elijah Muhammad's teachings into my own consciousness I knew they were meant for others (Black people) but I felt they applied to me too. It was like being between two shores; while the message spoke to black people in its own way, it spoke to white people in another. I understood white people collectively as "devils" (the name by which he called Caucasians), but personally I knew I wasn't one. I never felt Elijah Muhammad offended me for telling the truth; I felt he saved me from falsehood. Very few Whites, if any, ever gave Elijah Muhammad credit for providing them with a psychoanalysis of themselves. During a time when white sociologists and psychologists were having a heyday conducting the studies of Black people, Elijah Muhammad had the nerve and insight to present an etiological study of the white man in his examination and diagnosis of the BLACKMAN IN AMERICA.*

He provided an explanation of the white man's origin, his nature, and his probable doom. I saw this as a blessing bestowed by him rather than an indictment, for no one had clearly explained the white man to himself. Elijah Muhammad, following the instructions of his teacher, W. Fard Muhammad, went to the very origins (root) of white pathology (white supremacy).

It is time that the white man and woman in America consider the evidence that was offered in these teachings of Elijah Muhammad. They have been in existence over a half of a century now and white people as a whole still refuse to confront their human afflictions. This message and all its implications must now reach across centuries of blocked passages and blind cui de sacs so that European- descended people can see themselves in an Africentric, indeed a universalistic, way, and ultimately connect themselves to an origin point. Once white people can embrace Black origination, they can embrace themselves in a true way, realizing that none of their progeny, ancestry nor civilization has autonomy nor originality, but lies firmly on the face of original people grounded in ancient Africa (Kemet) before Egypt was Egypt, and long before the Bible's Adam and Eve.

The following is a message of liberation that I have for all those still clinging to white supremacy, and to all those trying to rid themselves of it.

In his OUR SAVIOR HAS ARRIVED, Elijah Muhammad referred to a forthcoming book to be entitled "Black and White." Apparently it was never completed.

CHAPTER ONE

WHITE SUPREMACY
AND THE REJECTION OF HISTORY

Through the years I have often wondered about white people and their attitude towards history. I particularly became interested while teaching college classes. I could see the multitude of problems that would arise for the white student as compared to the black student.

For the black students, most of whom had been denied access to their history through inadequate schooling still controlled by white Eurocentric thinking, the discovery of great black civilizations, beautiful traditions, ancient religion, honorable ancestors, and indeed, the very origins of life itself, as their own heritage was truly uplifting and inspiring for them. But for white students, this excavation into the past, which would uproot and expose the prevaricated history they had believed all along, proved to be the most painful. The amount of discomfort seemed to prevent most of them from continuing any kind of prolonged and serious probing of history that went beyond the usual Eurocentric survey courses and Western historical literature.

In probing the annals of American and European history my white students commonly say: "Why bring up all that old race stuff, today is another day," or "what good is it to keep looking at the past, all that is over, it doesn't have anything to do with today." Here are some examples: A student commented after the class had seen the movie "Black History: Lost, Stolen, or Strayed:"

"Yes, black history should be remembered (black men lost in history, etc.) but not to be shown or reminded of what white ancestors did to them. We can't apologize forever for what our ancestors did; it's not our fault. Also this film was twenty years ago, although some things pertain, blacks also have more opportunities than then."

The following is a typical example of a white student's reaction to the present because he/she has no real grasp of the past:

"They (Blacks) say they just want to be equal. They have their own exclusive magazines (EBONY, JET, etc.) and T.V. shows (Soul Train, Black Entertainment, etc.). But if the white people had a magazine called Ivory, we would be discriminating against the Blacks. That I don't understand. That I have a problem with. We have white institutions but we do not exclude the Black. We don't call them 'white' institutions."

And the usual response that everything is all right now and the past is past, gone, and has no relevance to today:

"I feel that our society had made up for and gives all Afro-Americans the chance to better themselves or be as equal to whites. I feel that the way Afro-Americans were treated they believe that they will never be equal. If they were paid back in full for the past, what would they have to compete with? If some minority Afro-American groups concentrated more on the increasing opportunities they have and took advantage of them, rather than competing and complaining for more of their success, that point would be crossed, and they might recognize all that our society has done to better the laws, benefits, and opportunities for them so that they couldn't continue putting down the society."

This Ignorance and rejection of history allows Whites to continue in illusions of greatness and white supremacy that can only be eliminated by 'unfolding the layers of rejected history. What most white people fail to understand is that they too have been denied access to the true history which undergirds their present life, and in the absence of truth fail to gain knowledge of themselves. In rejecting the truth of "Black history" (all the way back to beginnings) they have rejected the truth of themselves and the crucial key to unlocking the doors to both the past and present, and therefore, any clear path towards the future.

I am convinced that the only way for present generations of white people to transcend a legacy of white supremacy and false consciousness is to embrace and pursue with passion the historical endeavor. It is not about saying "we're all equal now, forget the past." It is not about "liking" and "accepting" contemporary Blacks. It is about accepting the past and being able to search the past for knowledge which explains and accounts for current behaviors.

When James Baldwin said in his *Rap On Race* with Margaret Mead: "the key to the salvation of America lies in whether or not it is able to embrace the black face,"' I don't think he meant to grab your black friend and kiss him or her; he meant: embrace the truth of blackness, in order to see the truth of whiteness; embrace the black face in order to see one's own countenance on the arc of history. Baldwin was speaking of a mental move; a heartfelt determination to uncover the layers of pastness that somehow has shielded the white mind from the truth of itself.

In *The Fire Next Time*, Baldwin said: "Caucasians are, in effect, still trapped in a history which they do not understand; and until they understand it, they cannot be released from it."[1] ¯

What history are Caucasians trapped in then? It is an historical vacuum; a chunk of time which has been severed from its origin point and reconstructed in terms of fabricated accounts and falsified documents. Such an historical and truncated worldview has allowed the illusion of white supremacy to become not only a general mindset, but an insidious underlying strategy which informs and constitutes every institution within American society (or the dominant white society anywhere in the universe).

This mindset, which has no grounding in the origins of human presence, no recognized connection to the first civilizations of human being nor the wisdom accumulated in those civilizations (except for what was stolen and/or rethought and rewritten) is a mindset trapped. For human understanding is exactly what it says: standing under the human, referring by reflection to that which accounts for and explains the very structure of life in which people exist. Trapped history is history without a naval cord to its very being, absent the mother of its inception. That is the foundation of white supremacy.

While the Europeans took what they needed and wanted from the original people in Africa to form the foundations of Western civilization, they simultaneously denied and rejected that very source. What occurred was a deliberate effort to cover up, conceal and alter the true origins of human life, in order to establish a supremacist worldview and eventually a civilization which recognized no liability for or answerability to the laws of nature embedded in the universe as well as in human nature. In no way is this better illustrated than the

European's calculations to sever the connection to the true ancient source by using (misusing) scripture to back up their false claims.

THE COVER UP OF ORIGINS:
DISINFORMATION ON GENESIS AND JESUS

It all goes back to beginnings; the American public school system would never be in the ridiculous position it now finds itself concerning" Evolution vs. Creation," if it had the possession of correct history Nor would it still be besieged by racism both in curricula and human relations.

Essentially, what occurred over a period of time in the effort to dissociate Western civilization and its institutions from the original peoples and civilizations who were the source and inspiration for its foundation, was a collaboration to fabricate the origins story, and thus establish the European (the white man) as the original human.

The spate of contemporary research and literature now forming a clear and more accurate vision of the actual origin point for world civilizations and the errors of European history, has come forth primarily in the 1970's and 80's, in the work of anthropologists, archaeologists, and historians, such as L.S.B. Leakey, Chiek Anta Diop, Asa Hilliard, Ivan van Sertima, Yosef ben-Yochanon, Charles Finch, Tony Browder and others But the Hon. Elijah Muhammad boldly declared the problem in *Message to the Blackman,* published in 1965 (actually he taught the contents of Message in the twenty years or so preceding in his oral deliveries and newspaper articles).

Quite logically, his book addresses the nature of Allah (God) first and then proceeds to the section on "original man." In clarion words, he declared:

The original man, Allah has declared, is none other than the black man. The black man is the first and last, maker and owner of the universe. From him came all brown, yellow, red and black people. By using a special method of birth control law the black man was able to produce the white race.[2]

Because Elijah Muhammad's teachings were spiritually

inspired with open reference to Allah repeatedly, and they had no lengthy footnotes attached, no references to the academic scholarship which had prevailed surrounding the question of origins, academics across the nation and world would dismiss him and remain secure in the Eurocentric perspective which dominated all institutions of learning. But it is known that governmental officials and informants to the controlling powers in the United States did not dismiss him so lightly and actually continued surveillance all through his public life as head of the Nation of Islam. After all, he was calling for an expose the like of which had never been sought before:

The time has arrived when it must be told the world over. There are millions who do not know who is the original man. Why should this question be put before the world today? Because it is the time of judgement between the black and white and the knowledge of the rightful owners of the earth. [3]

Elijah Muhammad's account of the original man and the subsequent "making" of the white man was transmitted to him by the one called Mahdi, W. Fard Muhammad. It essentially stipulated that one of the original men, called Yakub, produced the white race. Having mastered the studies available in the institutions of learning at his time (about 6,600 years ago), Yakub concentrated on the study of the life germ of man. By grafting the weaker gene, he would arrive at the white race, a new race he envisioned as ruling over all others, thus the making of the "devil" and unrighteous rule which would last about 6,000 years.

Elijah Muhammad counseled black people to "accept their own," to love self and quit following and mimicking white people:

To accept your own means yourself and your kind, your God Who is of you and you are of Him. It was your fathers who created the heavens and the earth, while there is nothing the white man has created independently. He did not even create himself. The Black Nation is self-created, while the white race is made by one of the gods and scientists of the Black nation. Their time on our planet is nothing compared to the time that we have been in the universe on this planet. It is hardly a fraction of a minute if we divide their 6,000 years into our billions and trillions of years. It would run into little or no time at all." [4]

In summary, what Elijah Muhammad declared was that the original man reached far back into time, past the genealogies of the book of Genesis: "the black nation has no birth record."[5]

A decade later, noted anthropologist and archaeologist L.S.B. Leakey said much the same thing as Elijah Muhammad, only in different words, delivered in a scientific lecture called "Progress of Man in Africa: "

> *...men of science today are with few exceptions satisfied that Africa was the birthplace of man himself...*
> *Africa's first contribution to human progress, then, was the evolution of man himself.*[6]

In 1987, the controversial genetic analysis of Mark Stoneking and Rebecca Cann (University of California, Berkeley) appearing in the January issue of *Nature* magazine, corroborated the fundamental teaching of Elijah Muhammad. The analysis was in keeping with the prevailing anthropological/archaeological conclusions that modern forms of *homo sapiens*, the species to which all living people belong, arose more than 100,000 years ago in Africa, only the Berkeley scientist put the date back to 200,000 years ago and identified the mitochondrial DNA's (genes) of the 147 people studied as stemming from one common ancestor, a maternal ancestor in Africa. Thus, the genetic "base," the primary matter of human life arose in the dark space of a black woman's womb, in the dark vastness of the African continent (before it was known as Africa).

This common maternal ancestor is now referred to as the African Eve by researchers, and how far back her genetic line extends into the origins of life itself we do not know. The dates above refer to direct ancestors of modern man, but the actual age of the life-germ is unrecorded, not known. But one thing we do know is that African Eve surely deviates from the Eurocentric version and imaging of the biblical Eve in Genesis, who is presented as a European prototype placed in the Garden of Eden by a God who seems to work against His own natural order by placing Adam and Even there fully mature and without any connection to the long evolution of human life itself. The biblical Eve is seen as an afterthought, and a bad one at that; but African Eve as presented by the Berkeley researchers is seen as primal and essential to the life process itself .

There have been many others through the years who have discovered and named various human ancestors (hominids) through archaeological procedures and fossil analysis. Donald Johanson, a paleoanthropologist, brought " Lucy" to the long line of descent. Her bones found in northern Ethiopia, she was labeled *afarensis* as a hominid species and speculated to be about 3.5 million years old. There was controversy and doubt over Lucy in the '70's just as there has been over African Eve in the '80'5. But the accumulated evidence overall through the various disciplines is too convincing and overwhelming for there not to be a general atmosphere of consensus and acceptance by the scientific community. The late Cheikh Anta Diop, called the "pharoah of African studies" by Van Sertima, concludes his brilliant paper on Africa as the cradle of humanity, with these words: ". ..from 5 million years ago to the glacial thaw 10,000 years ago, Africa almost unilaterally peopled and influenced the rest of the world." [7]

Of course, neither the Leakeys nor Stoneking and Cann; not Johanson or any of the others, ever tell us anything about Yakub. But I felt Yakub's presence in their findings. That is to say, I could "feel" in my mind the divergence of a genetic wholeness as the Caucasian or European presence began to appear in human history. Indeed, the *human* quality of this people's deeds seemed almost completely absent.

A young black woman student asked me one day after class: "Do you believe the Yakub story about white people?" I answered in the way I answered myself, it made sense to me. But I couldn't provide myself or her with proof of Yakub from anthropological, archaeological, nor historical literature, except as it appeared between the lines, in the unspoken yet worded narrative of the human species evolution. What I realized in my first acquaintance with the teachings of Elijah Muhammad was that they provided a link to a mysterious void and abyss in the knowledge of myself and the ancient world beyond my grasp. The more I reflected on his account of the making of the white man, the more it seemed accurate. I could see the "genetic weakness" in my own race. There were case histories of Europeans being unable to withstand the elements of sun and heat. But the black man could be put anywhere on earth and he would survive. I began to notice more and more the characteristic of the European or white world history. Nowhere on earth have they traveled but they wreaked havoc upon indigenous populations.

Michael Bradley in *The Iceman Inheritance,* presents extensive research that demonstrates western or caucasoid man's extreme aggression. He attributes this behavior to the thesis that only Caucasoids " crossed the *sapiens* threshold in a glacial environment." This, according to Bradley, led to maladaptions psychobiologically for the Caucasoid type, resulting in overly aggressive behavior, a mindset which generated future-limiting mechanisms, and patholoical sexual-sensual adaptations among other things. [8]

While I think Bradley's work is somewhat western culture-bound in its analyses, we may be talking about the same "genetic shortage" I mentioned above. I am more inclined to look for evidence of Yakub as Elijah Muhammad described him, thus including a more conscious element in the deviating trajectory of the white man surrounding his origins. Also, Bradley sees the Caucasoid behavior as having "scarred the earth" for 30,000 years. One might dispute that the Western man has "ruled" that long; Elijah Muhammad put it closer to 6,600 years, with some extension of his rule reaching into present time.

Now with the increasing amount of information coming out on the factor of melanin in one's system, I am led to believe this "shortage" has to do with the lack of melanin. It remains to be seen just what the overall function of melanin is and how it might account for the divergent behavior patterns of the Aryan or white, European type of human. Melanin, in essence then, could be seen as the humanizing factor. [9]

So, in my classes, even though I could provide some impressive evidence for African or Black origins, I could only speculate about white beginnings if I wanted to refer to scientific data. I could, however, simply narrate the account provided by Elijah Muhammad, and leave it at that. The essential factor in all of the material was that black was first, and white presence depended on black originality. Put another way, white was simply the appearance of the lack of melanin.

I can recall an anthropology text book some ten or fifteen years ago (the title since lost to my memory) which featured the tree of life or mankind. In typical Eurocentric supremacist fashion, it placed the white race as the trunk of the tree and all other races as branches spreading out from the trunk. I presented this racist version of the tree of life to my class in a university, then turned it around, placing the black race as the trunk and all other so-called races as branches from the trunk. In fact, I put the white race as a very weak, deviating kind of thin offshoot appearing higher up (much later) than the other larger limbs (other races). I asked the students what they thought as I interspersed the diagram with some teachings of Elijah Muhammad. Being mostly white students, they either were shocked and silent, or found it amusing and dismissed it as some kind of wild theory I personally conjured up. Today this little exercise in anthropological analysis would be called "reverse racism." But of course it isn't. It is the unmitigated truth. Most Whites never seem to realize that if their ancestors switched the true colors of origins around, to restore the rightful hue to its primary place is not reverse racism but a correction in historical error.

Likewise, the Eurocentric version of the Genesis story has altered the truth of origins, and in doing so has generated n intellectual scandal in the public schools, subjecting young people to a confusing " argument" between so-called theories, both of which are erroneous and totally irrelevant to any kind of authentic understanding of origins. The basic extremes of the Creationism vs Evolutionism argument are:

1)   *that creation means a "special creation" in which man (perceived as the ultimate in creation) is specially designed by a creator, apparently outside the laws of nature which would require stages of growth, that is, a form of evolution.*

2) *that man developed in a random, almost accidental evolutionary process from lower life to a present kind of higher human life, with no reference to creator or recognizable order.* [10]

Neither of these views offers a child in school much of a choice. The young mind is presented with mutually exclusive theories and textbook arguments which provide no inwardly satisfying conclusions about the origins of human life.

Creation and evolution need not be mutually exclusive. That all things in the universe mature through stages is an open, visible, observable law which we cannot deny. Therefore, evolution, growth through stages, is a given. The Our'an says: "It is He that beginneth the process of creation." (Surah X: 14)

Creation implies intent: creator. It implies that every aspect of the world we live in reveals order, design, pattern {or the deviation and erratic straying from such order). Even the process of change from one form of life to another involves a design: when one thing becomes another, it is *time* for mutation or transferal. When a fetus is ready for light, another environment, it demands to come out into light. (God said: let there be light and there was) When a caterpillar needs to become a butterfly, it breaks out, mutates the form. When hominidae (the precursors to modern man) reached *homo sapiens,* it was time. One form becomes another. It becomes (Be and it is). This divine command is an inward, immanent thing. The problem with the Western version of creation and evolution is: creator is perceived as apart from and external to the created, or process of creation. It is a "super" natural event, a "super" natural entity that makes things apart from it and outside the bonds of natural law (which presumably this entity also created).

The true language of creation implies inwardness, immanence. The Creator wills from within, and it *becomes* and *is.* Westerners look for external events that can be marked as the point when such and such occurred. They view the process of creation as a once and for-all event which established the primacy of man on earth; this made- man did not have to struggle and move through the process of becoming. He was just made and put here, like a cut-out paper doll. A student recently expressed this mentality in the following statement:

I believe there is a God, a creator of the world, but once He did, that was it—He has nothing else to do with it. Man makes his own world and messes it up.

This not uncommon mixture of truth and falsehood emphasizes that a God " external" to the world made it and left it on its own, has nothing to do with it "anymore." Such thinking separates Creator and created in a way that the created manifests no attributes of godliness, is accountable to no higher power or law other than his own argument that further conceals the discovery of origins. None today, unless we are octogenarians, can "remember" how the -up began --just when and where the gradual rearranging of occurred. But we have a record. It is embedded in the lines of n history, between the lines of written history, and of course lost in the pages of unwritten history. Even so, the earth has a way elching up" , as the Qur'an says, its entrails and from time to things come to light, like the Qumran Scrolls and the remains cient ancestors fossilized. If we ask the right questions and nstrate a searing desire to get through to the actuality of what down, we will be able to comprehend.

We know, for example, that Archbishop James Ussher placed eation or beginning of the world at 4004 B.C. with Adam. Why e do this? Who was he and how did he arrive at his figure? It is hat this was how he calculated the dates expressed in scripture. er was an Anglican primate of Ireland and in 1607 became the rofessor of Divinity at Dublin, about the time King James I of nd had assembled his 54 scholars to produce the "King James on" of the Bible (which would first appear in 1611). Ussher's dar of the creation or beginning of the world and subsequent s appeared in altered versions, starting in 1701, it is reported.[11]

By placing Adam at 4004 B.C. Ussher safely situated the first outside the scope of the most ancient African civilization and but comfortably within European civilization (which dates 6,000 years old). In classes, when I try to reconstruct the actu-ronology of modern man *(homo sapiens)* as he emerged or ed from an origin point of at least two to three million years ago oint out the Bishop's outstanding error, students will inevitably that scientists hadn't at the time been able to establish the age manity via technical means such as radiocarbon dating, etc. So ishop was innocent.

While it is true that major archaeological and biochemical veries have occurred mostly in the 19th and 20th Centuries, I not let the Bishop off so easily. All we have to do is expose p Ussher in the total social context of his time to understand his

24

"error."

Consider the following: The Portuguese were involved in the enslavement of Africans as early as 1411. Spain was early into the African slave traffic over one hundred years before Ussher was even born. In 1441 Antam Gonsalves brought back "negroes" from West Africa it is reported. In 1517, Charles V began to issue license for the importation of African slaves in the West Indies.

In other words, the European "civilization" totally controlled by its religious institution in the form of the Roman Catholic Church, entered into deliberate and continuous invasion of other peoples, as well as the enslavement of many of their populations. All the way to the Assiento, a kind of tri-party agreement between the Church, Spain and England, to allow the latter to have her part of the slave trade, the major European powers were about the business of colonizing, enslaving and exterminating, all with the blessing of the Church.[12]

The infamous John Hawkins, operating in the service of England and Queen Elizabeth, knew a good thing when he saw it. His greed to cash in on the lucrative traffic in black flesh led him to vie with the Spanish for some share of the trade in the 1560's. As comptroller of the English Navy and having authority with the nation's treasury, he pursued this vicious traffic in cargoes of Black people, wearing a crest (like a coat of arms) which featured the image of a black man bound in a cord. Hawkins defeated the Spanish Armada in 1588, three years after Ussher was born. He died in his memorable expedition off Puerto Rico in 1595 when his tricks and deception in dealing with the Spanish finally caught up with him.[13]

Now we can see Bishop Ussher in the total picture. It was only eight years following Hawkins' death that King James ordered a new version of the Bible. Obviously, all those collaborating on the right "version" of the scriptural presentation were quite familiar with the African slave traffic and the continent from which they came. That these men were totally unaware of the utter age of African civilizations, whether in the lower region around the Nile cradle and valley, or over on the West Coast and interior where slaves were captured, is doubtful. In short, the dilemma they faced was: how do you give a beginning to man—and the black man is found to be older than yourself, and this very black man is being identified as less than man, for the purpose of enslavement and economic profiteering?

Bishop Ussher was reported to be a scholar and authority on the Letters of St. Ignatius of Antioch. Antioch was a gateway from the ancient Egyptian (African) world to the Greek world, to the West. Antioch was a place where early "Christianity" flourished and where dissent would become a major threat to "the Church." There is a shroud of mystery around Ussher: how much did he know of the connection between Jesus and Egypt? Between the Greeks and Egypt? Surelya man of Ussher's stature, with his vast study, research and biblical expertise would have some knowledge of the ancient civilization established in Africa. Su rely he would have read the classics and especially Herodotus, who says in Book II, 16:

> *I do not believe that the Egyptians came into being at the same period as the Delta; on the contrary, they have existed ever since mankind appeared on earth, and as the Delta increased with the passage of time, many of them moved into the new territory and many remained where they originally were.*[14]

By now we can see even a larger picture in which to cast Ussher, James and all others involved with the origins cover-up. That picture involves an earlier cover-up: the disinformation on Jesus. Before the call for a new biblical version in the 17th Century, and before Bishop Ussher delivered his calendar of the creation of the world, there had been 17 centuries of cover-up surrounding Jesus, and the true history surrounding Egypt, more properly identified as Kemet.

Although the Greeks (reportedly the founders of Western philosophy and civilization) had begun their grand theft of ancient Egyptian (African) knowledge some 500 to 300 years before Jesus, the elimination of Jesus as one who was familiar with the ancient Kemetic mystery system by "losing" the major portion of his life and then elevating him to the status of the trinitarian God, the establishers of the church and Roman Empire managed to bring about a total severance of the European world from ancient Africa.[15]

The controversy over Jesus dominated the church for the first centuries after Jesus' death. Only in Jesus' death and departure could the enemies of him complete their usurpation of ancient knowledge for themselves (to later be stored and codified under Freemasonry).

They did this by making him " of the same substance as God," that is, *homo-ousian)*. The controversy raged between the eastern and western blocs of the church. Enter Arius.

Arius, described as "tall, handsome, ascetic, earnestly religious, an eloquent preacher," was a presbyter in the Alexandrian church (that is, the community which had been renamed under Alexander in his invasion and conquest of northern Africa).[16] He was said to be from Libya, therefore not of the western branch of the newly forming "church." It is probable that he saw Jesus in the light of ancient wisdom that was the womb of "education" for all the early religious figures as well as for the scholars. Self-knowledge was the aim of religion.

Rev Charles Potter says of Arius:

"...He received his education in that Antioch of Syria where the disciples of Jesus were first called Christians, probably because of their Essenic emphasis on the Messianic-Christian doctrine of the Coming Kingdom of God and the Son of Man.

Antioch was important in Arius's education, for there he sat under the teaching of the great Presbyter Lucian, a very learned man and noted scholar who revised the Greek Septuagint Old Testament by comparison with the Hebrew text. And Lucian was, in turn, a follower of Paul of Samosata, the famous "heretical" Patriarch and Bishop of Antioch, excommunicated by seventy bishops, priests, and deacons for teaching that Jesus was a man who became God, rather than a God who became man." [17]

The heresy of this patriarch was the view of Jesus as simply a man, but one who attained such a degree of holiness, he was adopted as a son of God. Those adhering to such a view were said to endorse a doctrine of " Adoptianism." Around Antioch this view was common place. Jesus was man. A highly perfected man.

Arius continued in this tradition arguing that God only is without beginning, and the son is not a part of God. Thus his statement: "We confess one God, who alone is unbegotten, alone eternal, alone without beginning, alone true, alone possessing immortality, alone wise and good."[18]

Arius was banished to Gaul in 335 A.D., ten years after the great Council at Nicea, 325, that momentous "summit" that issued the most critical "white paper" of all time perhaps, the Nicene Creed which established Jesus as *homo-ousian*, a member of the Trinity, god incarnate. After Constantine's death, Arius returned again for a time, and Arianism in its total movement posed a great threat to the western Church and Empire. Arianism was, afterall, monotheism, and it was hard to put down the Arian view, beings it was the view of ancient Kemet, originating from the most ancient of peoples and time. The Arians were very close to creating an Arian state, "which would have given a decidedly different story to the history of the Church," says Glanville Downey, writing on ancient Antioch.[19]

Bishop Ussher, as a scholar on Ignatius of Antioch, would have had to be well acquainted with this pivotal moment in the direction of the early Christian Church. Antioch was a bridge you could say from the ancient religious traditions of the past. It was the center of monotheistic theological thought. This is better understood once the connection is made to ancient Egypt and its longstanding (longer than the Hebrews even) adherence to monotheism, and the Kemetic Mystery system which revolved around the initiation of its priests into the studies which would build, degree by degree, the perfection of the self into a holy and enlightened being.

How much Ussher investigated and understood the ancient Kemetic tradition of self-mastery that preceded western Christianity seems to be lost in the pages of history. Ussher, along with all the theologians seems to either have ignored or rejected not only the true genealogy of Jesus but all the Old Testament figures, safely establishing them as the originators of the human family and out of the scope of ancient African religion and cultural history.

Dr. Charles Finch, for example, has spoken in television interviews on the meaning of the name " Abraham." Breaking it down into *Ab ra him* the meaning results in "desire of the light of the sun." Finch also has stated that Egyptians believed Moses to be a renegade Egyptian priest who took a group out of Egypt.[20] This view of Moses would have some affinity for Elijah Muhammad's teaching that Moses was in fact sent to the "devil" to try to raise him (the white race that is) from the uncivilized state and condition he found him in, in the caves of Europe.

By making Jesus "superhuman," out of the realm of natural law (from his virgin birth to his ascension, all interpreted physically) the formulators of Western theology and civilization deprived the masses of people of the knowledge which would have been the key to unlocking the depth of themselves and the way to self- mastery. Jesus was stopped in his mission because he was sharing the keys to the Kingdom of God, the kingdom being, just as he said, "within." Immanence. He was showing people how to perfect and trust their own powers. The Essenes, a religious community Jesus seems to have been associated with, have a definite, direct relationship to the ancient Egyptian Mystery system.[21]

It should be plain now why the hidden years, the lost years of Jesus were in fact obscured from Western civilization, why his own identity as a non-European was completely distorted and whitened until Ussher's calendar of creation seemed plausible. There had been numerous exchanges between Semitic and African peoples before Moses, and Jesus came after Moses some 1500 years. Cheikh Anta Diop says Moses went up to Mt. Sinai at the end of the 12th Dynasty (Egyptian) in 1491 B.C. It seems quite plausible that a man of Jesus' wisdom would know about that ascent. After all, twelve dynasties had already come and gone by Moses' time; and the Ptolemies (Greeks) had come to power in Egypt by Jesus' time, ending with Cleopatra 30 years before Jesus was allegedly born, born in Palestine where Africans had long resided. Jesus was of the original people. Says Professor Geoghagan in his informing and definitive interview on Jesus: " Jesus was a black man."[22]

Is it not clear now why Western historians have separated Jesus from the political reality of Africa? Surely Jesus and others around Palestine, which had been inhabited by Africans for years, knew of Alexander's military expeditions into Africa only 300 years prior to Jesus' birth. Surely they knew of the Greek Ptolemies and the take over by the Romans. And surely Jesus knew he was not "of the Romans," and he knew what it was to live in "occupied territory" just as Palestinians do today.

So who was Jesus of? The original peoples, and the ancient African religious knowledge that had been taught to "initiates" for centuries --for at least 4,000 years -- (the 4,000 stolen from Africa and given to Europe). Just as Moses got his ten commandments from the African Constitution, Jesus was instructed in the most ancient of ways.[23] Rev. Potter points out: "It was not a long journey between

Alexandria and Jerusalem, and was particularly cheap and pleasant by sea, so it is very likely that the two Essene communities (in Alexandria and Jerusalem) exchanged books and visits."[24]

Jesus was most likely a member of the Jerusalem Essene group. It is possible that Philo, who lived in Alexandria and wrote *Every Virtuous Man Is Free* and *Concerning The Contemplative Life*, was not all that unknown to Jesus nor Jesus to him. Says Potter:

> **By this line of communication, Philo's books could easily have come into the hands of Jesus in Palestine, whether he was in an Essene community there or not.**[25]

Somehow a myth arose in later years that Jesus could not have known Greek; and of course the King James version of the Bible came from the Greek version, and it purged the scripture of many of the books in earlier versions, called the apocrypha, which later surfaced in the Qumran Scrolls.

For the Romans, Jesus was much safer as *homo-ousian* (part of the same substance, part of the Trinity we could say) than as *homoi-ousian* (of like substance). that is as a perfected and holy man. Once the Church "captured" Jesus in a wafer of bread, called the host, and fed him to the people, who believed that by swallowing "the body of Christ" they would be purified, the church and government authorities would continue to have unlimited power over the people. The wafer was an alien object, an external item which by entering the body cleansed and protected it from itself. Gone was the ancient mystery system whereby one would appeal to the natural laws governing self and universe as keys to mastery of the self and thus salvation.

What was dangerous about leaving Jesus human? What was dangerous about leaving him alive? His teachings were from that ancient way which was a well-defined and practiced system of "ordering one's life." By knowing the make-up of the self--the laws of the physical, emotional and spiritual realms --one could master the self and thus attain liberation and the means whereby one could confront and reject all those who attempted to control and oppress the self.

Essentially, what "Christianity" did was generate a civilization built on the false premise that man is born in sin and needs a savior, other than the divinity within the self, in order to be saved. This placed something in between self and God. By misinterpreting Genesis and misidentifying Jesus, the founders of Western civilization were able to keep hidden from the masses of people the very knowledge which would set them free.

All that remained was for the rulers to whiten up the biblical lIstories" in order to demonstrate who was in power. Once the true identity of Jesus was obscured, the Western theologians and historians could continue to whiten the history of Egypt and establish the Greeks as the foundation of "civilized" life.

Chancellor Williams. in his *Destruction of Black Civilization,* points out that even in recent years an African History published by the American Historical Association to serve as a guide for teaching history, was carefully arranged to exclude Black Africa from its own making. This version places the first period of African history from the Fall of the Roman Empire to 700 A.D., the time of the so-called Arab invasions; the second period is stated to be the Islamic period from 700 A.D. to 1500; the third period was European from 1500 to 1960, with a subdivision at 1880 to mark colonialism. Williams concludes: "There is no period of Black civilization in Black Africa!" This Eurocentric version eliminates 4,000 years of Black civilization and the greatest periods of African achievements.[26]

It is this same 4,000 years I believe the European Biblical scholars and religious figures have stolen and identified as their own. The old ancients of the Bible such as Adam and Abraham and Moses were eventually Europeanized so that they were always interpreted as the precursors or ancestors of the white baby Jesus (as he later became portrayed in biblical art), rather than as the descendants and heirs of Black civilization. This brings to mind a memory of my childhood when we would be arranging the manger at Christmas time. There was one black figuring among the wise men as I recall, and he was always seen (by me at least) as being a "foreigner"-- one who traveled the most miles to see Jesus. Having grown up in Kentucky during segregation, that was like the Blacks (Negroes) who came to see the new white baby born to Missus. He was never interpreted as Jesus' kin or being of a royal family.

George G. M. James *(Stolen Legacy)* clearly demonstrates the final severance of the Christian West from its mother , the Ancient

Egyptian Mystery religion when he refers to the edicts of Emperors Theodosius in the 4th Century A.D. and Justinian in the 6th, as abolishing the Mysteries of the African Continent, thus the ancient culture system of the world. Justinian as Roman Emperor abolished the Temples and schools of philosophy associated with the Greeks (who stole the knowledge from the Egyptians).[27]

Robin Lane Fox identifies the ancient Egyptian source and its Greek imitations as "pagan" and devotes some 700 pages in his PAGANS AND CHRISTIANS to documenting the "shift" from "paganism to Christianity." The truth peeps out between the lines. Justinian might have abolished the philosophical circles who were carrying on the wisdom, but he confiscated the ancient gods all the same. When he founded a new city in Christian North Africa in honor of his wife, Theodora, a mosaic floor there revealed the spring of Delphi, and four streams of Wisdom now identified as Christian rivers of Paradise, but in fact the rivers of ancient knowledge coming from the four corners of the universe. [28]

Of course Fox and others have misidentified the pagans. Ancient Egyptians were not paganistic, but monotheistic, recognizing the "godliness" of its human creatures as they personified the emanations of the One. They, like the Native Americans, have been accused of "polytheism," because westerners misunderstood the great respect each had for universal laws and natural phenomena.

The cover-up took on momentum when the images began to proliferate making Jesus and all Biblical figures appear to be European, that is, white. It is noteworthy that the first Virgin Mother and Child images arose out of ancient Kemet and the early African-based Christianity, before the Roman Church captured the idea of the Madonna and Child. In his Introduction to Cheikh Anta Diop's *The Cultural Unity of Black Africa*, John Henrik Clarke describes this metamorphosis from black Madonnas to the more Europeanized versions, by pointing out that the virgin mother and child appeared in more ancient forms. There was the North African Ast or Isis in Greek, who gave birth to Heru or Horus. As a black Madonna, Isis was seen in temples in Africa, Spain, Italy and France. The Great Cathedral of Notre Dame in Paris is supposed to be built on the site of an earlier shrine of the Black Madonna. Clarke says it was only after the Council of Ephesus in 481 that the Virgin Mary and Child became the symbols of Christianty. Madonnas then began to spread in Europe, most of them black. They were enshrined at Loretto, Orapa, Genoa, Pisa, and Padua. Switzerland displays one in Einsiedein. [29]

In 660 A.D. Pope Gregory is reported to have introduced picture books for illiterates to replace the Bible. It should be noted that Prophet Muhammad shortly thereafter would be combatting idolatry also in Mecca. Islam, the "way" of life being delivered by Muhammad was about bringing people back to the worship of one God. In other words, he knew what had happened to Jesus as icons took on a power akin to God's in the minds of the people. In Mecca idols were already under attack.

This controversy over the use of images among the Church hierarchies raged for several centuries, just as the controversy over the nature of Jesus did. And it would, like the first controversy, culminate in a councilor synod at the Seventh Council of Nicea. According to Encyclopedia Britannica (Macropedia Vol. 4) in the western church, images were viewed as the Holy Scriptures, a substitute for the illiterate. Thus images became a bible for the laity. Notice there was no literacy campaign to teach the people how to read, but a strategy whereby they could be pacified and remain powerless. Jesus had taught that knowledge would set one free, and some five centuries later Muhammad declared the first revelation of the Holy Qu'ran: "Read! In the Name of the Lord! " Prophet Muhammad began his effort to rid the Kaaba of images and false idols, spreading the message to the people, urging them to read nature (signs in nature) and whatever else they could to gain knowledge.

The Church, however, continued to use imagery as a powerful psychological tool to capture the minds and hearts of the masses of people, binding them to mental pictures of Europeanized {white) holy figures and the divine figures of the Christ. White supremacy in essence depended on visual aids in establishing its primacy in the collective psyche.

Pope Gregory II in the Bth Century opposed the eastern (Byzantine) Emperor, Leo III, who ordered all holy images to be destroyed. This was the launching of the iconoclastic controversy. The iconoclasts objected to the idols and images on the basis of the Old testament in the ten commandments (which, recall, came from the African Constitution) (See Ex 20:4). The defenders of image use insisted on their symbolic nature and the dignity of created matter. It was Empress Irene, a woman whose sentiments apparently had been moved by icons, who convened the 7th Ecumenical Council at Nicea and condemned the iconoclasts and re-established the use of images in the Church. And it was an emperor's widow who later restored icon veneration after the death of her husband, Theophilus.

The Western Church had prevailed once again, and a theology of images grew. Says the Encyclopedia Britannica, "The image of Christ, the incarnated God, became for Eastern Christians a pictorial confession of faith; God was truly visible in the humanity of Jesus of Nazareth and saints, whose images surround that of Christ."[30]

The use of images was even more strongly established in Church theology when Thomas Aquinas, the influential medieval theologian, identified the purpose of images:

1) for the instruction of the uneducated in place of books

2) for illustrating and remembering the mystery of the incarnation (God becoming flesh in Jesus)

3) for the awakening of the passion of devotion which is kindled more effectively on the basis of viewing than hearing.[31]

Aquinas pinpointed the very basis of the western worldview or axiology when he referred to passion. By feeding the appetite for immediate sentient gratification, he fundamentally gave a psychological directive for controlling and motivating the masses of uneducated people. Of course by this time Prophet Muhammad had been dead for sometime and had crushed any tendency to deify him by instructing his companions to never show images of his face (a principle followed to this day). Of course Islam was still spreading, and Christianity would fight it in the Crusades; two worldviews in confrontation: the Islamic with the focus on the inner reality; the Christian with focus on the outer (physical).

The use of imagery in falsifying and identifying holy personages and the deity has never been eliminated from the western Christian mindset. Western civilization became immersed in sentimental European versions of a frail and weakly appearing saviour and all his contemporaries were just as whitened and weakened until they became as vacuous and empty as the plastic versions of them in Christmas creches.

We can clearly understand now how white supremacy was dependent on and bolstered by the Church's use and abuse of imagery. As recently as the 1970's and '80's, one of the Muslim imams in America, Warith Deen Muhammad, has made continuous appeals to the American people, religious leaders and officials, to get rid of images which serve to uphold the pillars of white supremacy. Imam Muhammad's message was and is: you can't live in America and not hear the message of white supremacy. "You are conscious that Jesus is put into a white body even if you don't go to church. Every American knows that Jesus is put into a "white" European image by church society," says the Imam. His appeal has been to get rid of all racial images, stating that "the strongest wedge between non-Caucasians and Caucasians isa Caucasian symbolic image of God on the cross."[32]

Still, the use of imagery continues and all people in America and other sectors of the world touched and dominated by the Western mindset continue to be trapped in a history they do not know and mental pictures of holy imposters.

When we return to the question of origins, we can better understand what the context of the collective mind was of Europe at the time of Darwin and others immediately before and after him. By the 19th Century when the search for origins was underway by European Scientists, the primary godliness of white people had been secured in the fabricated imagery of the Christ and the holy saints surrounding him. Of course, it was the Europeans who pursued the search for origins because they were the only ones apparently who did not know their origins. Indigenous peoples everywhere else had ancient oral accounts of their beginnings (creation stories or Dreamtime).

Since the European creation story was embedded in the obscure and cryptic dual rendition presented in Genesis, which had its roots in more ancient stories coming from Kemet, little wonder was it that there would be scholars who doubted the fabrication and felt a genuine urge to return to the source and discover origins. Even so, despite their scientific departure from church theology, they surely were socialized into a culture of white supremacy. Thus, as I heard Dr. Asa Hilliard put it so well during one of his slide presentations: they (the Europeans) first looked for the oldest or the original man in Europe, and not finding him there, moved to Asia in hopes it would be found there, and finally had to go to Africa where of course the oldest remains were found. Darwin also foresaw that Africa most likely would be the origin point and indicated so.[33]

But others like Louis Agassiz, the Swiss born naturalist and zoologist who came to the United States and was based at Harvard, eventually establishing the Museum of Comparative Zoology and the Anderson School of Natural History, promulgated a "special" and separate origination of the races, so that he could comfortably hold on to the concept of a Divine Creator and at the same time maintain white supremacy. His biographer, Edward Luries, says:

Agassiz affirmed not only that Negroes and Whites were of distinct origins but also that Negroes were quite probably a physiologically and anatomically distinct species.[34]

This was his theory of "special creationism."

Lurie says the controversy over the unity of plurality of the human race had been of interest to Americans for many years. Agassiz became a very popular lecturer, even among lay people as well as academic circles. Dorothy Sterling refers to Agassiz in her book on black women in the 19th century and displays a picture of an African slave woman, one of many perhaps that Agassiz had photographed so he could make his "scientific comparisons." According to Sterling, Agassiz was able to get a southern plantation owner and slaveholder by the name of Taylor to order his slaves to pose nude for Agassiz' scientific theses. This took place around Charleston, S.C., the largest thriving slave-holding state in the South at one time.[35]

In the final analysis, we can now understand why science in the Western world became a realm unto itself, divorced from the reflective and intuitive disciplines of intellectual pursuit such as philosophy and theology. In the ancient world there were no such divisions of intellectual pursuit; knowledge was one and the ways to arrive at complete knowledge were to blend and interweave the various disciplines which involved knowing the physical and material as a basis for knowing the spiritual and inner realm of life itself. In the West, science becomes associated with a less than divinely inspired pursuit that threatens the pillars of theological revelation. In the ancient world, study of the universe's composition via the use of the various disciplines of liberal arts led to knowledge of the universe within (self-knowledge) as well as without. The theological and scientific were not at odds because neither was attempting to conceal, but rather reveal.

In the modern Western world science and religion are at odds because the latter has had the burden of perpetrating a lie since the establishment of the western church. This necessity to cover up and reject is the opposite of enlightenment, knowing and understanding. What the Scopes trial years later was all about, and what the evolution vs. creation controversy is about is not that man is connected to ape, but man (including the white man) is connected to Africa in origin. Despite the fact that *Newsweek, Nature,* and *National Geographic* have in the past five years alone published impressive feature articles on man's origins in Africa, there is still stubborn refusal on the part of many if not most whites to accept this evidence. It is much safer to retreat to a falsified biblical version of origins and remain truncated, mentally separated from the abyss of universal beginnings. The subtle deception in all of this is that Europeans associated African humans with apes and thus laid the basis for rejecting the white man's association with either.

The European had an incredible curiosity about the apes. They associated the *negro* and ape; they dissociated themselves. In his hallucinating supremacist mind, the European both feared and rejected the truth of origins. Still, he was driven to ask the question. African people never had this dilemma apparently. They knew who they were; they understood the nature of origins.

The English anatomist Tyson wrote an account of the man-like ape. It was the first such account with any pretensions of scientific accuracy. His treatise *Orangoutang, Sive Homo Sylvestris,* or: *The Anatomy of a Pygmy Compared With That of a Monkey, An Ape and a Man,* was published in 1699. Already devaluing the human quality of the pygmy, he voiced his suspicions: "The Pygmy does so much resemble a man... more than any of the ape kind, or any other animal in the world, that I know of; yet by no means do I look upon it as the product of a mixt generation." [36]

William Smith's *New Voyage to Guinea* came in 1744. White sailors, he reported, teased a slave about a she-cub (boggoe) after he had reprimanded them in some way for hurting the creature. They asked him if he didn't want it for his wife. The slave is reported to have replied: "No, this is no my wife. This is a white woman...that fit wife for you." The slave was found dead next morning." [37]

As Leakey pointed out years later, there never was any evidence of such close "kinship" between the great apes and man. "Near-man" types evolved as human species. It was the European in his mental hysteria who made the species associations as he dehumanized the African in his psyche and deified the European.

In the final analysis, European scientists could not be allowed (even in their own minds) to associate any white man with Africa in origins. Certainly not Jesus, who, recall, by this time had been safely relegated to the trinity status, and whitened in the images portrayed by European artists. Even in his human form, Jesus had to be generated from Jews, who were historically separated from black Africa by European scholars.

Who was the Jew? Cheikh Anta Diop answers:

What, then, was the Jewish people? How was it born? How did it create the Bible, in which descendants of Ham, ancestors of Negroes and Egyptians, would thus be accursed; what might be the historical reason for that curse? Those who would become the Jews entered Egypt numbering 70 rough, fearful shepherds, chased from Palestine by famine and attracted by that earthly paradise, the Nile Valley. [38]

Diop goes on to explain that the Jews, if persecuted there in Egypt, were thus so because of their possible proliferation and threat to the residents. If, he says, we are to believe the Bible, they were employed as laborers in construction work, building the city of Rameses. That they became a messianic suffering persecuted people was a natural response to an environment which increasingly seemed hostile yet far superior to their lack of social organization and industry. The Jews " armed with nothing but sticks could envisage no positive reaction to the technical superiority of the Egyptian people." Diop further says:

It was to meet this crisis that Moses appeared, the first of the Jewish prophets, who, after minutely working out the history of the Jewish people from its origins, presented it in retrospect under a religious perspective. Thus he caused Abraham to say many things that the latter could not have possibly foreseen; for example, the 400 years in Egypt.

In other words, Moses, living at the time of Tell el Amarna (a city above Cairo and new capital of Akhnaton's Empire) learned monotheism from the Egyptians. It was Akhnaton's efforts to revive monotheism that Moses was acquainted with. Says Diop: "Having entered Egypt as 70 shepherds grouped in 12 patriarchal families, nomads without industry or culture, the Jewish people left there 400 years later, 600,000 strong, after acquiring from it all the elements of its future tradition, including monotheism."[40]

According to Yosef ben-Jochannan, there is much to be questioned about Moses' authenticity as portrayed in scripture. In his work on Rameses II, Jochanan says:

What is conspicuously missing in all of the temples of Pharoah Rameses II, however, is the absence of any mention of a Haribu [Hebrew] people fleeing Ta-Meri [Ancient Egypt] from this or any other pharoah in what could be called an "exodus." For nowhere on any wall, ceiling, floor, column, statue, papyrus, obelisk, stela, and/or whatever else, is there any mention of Haribu (Haripu or Hebrew, Jewish) people. ...in any amount. ... even living in Ta-Meri during this period --the XIX Dynasty, ca. 1298-1232 B.C.E.--before, and/or after. [41]

Elsewhere Jochannan also shows what he calculates as a conflict of dates surrounding Moses, the Exodus, and Pharoah Rameses II. Moshe (Moses) supposedly is age 110 during 1298-1236 B.C. Rameses II reigns in 1298-1232, and Moses again supposedly disappearing in the Sinai during 1236- 1196. But the five books of Moses or Torah seem to appear closer to 700 B.C. Therefore, there is much dispute surrounding the person of Moses and Hebrews being slaves of the Pharoah. [42]

According to Diop, we can understand the curse of Ham {the negro or black Egyptian). It came from the Jew, not God. The curse fell only on Canaan who dwelt in a land that Jews had coveted throughout their history. Where did Ham come from? Right in Egypt, says Diop, from Cham (Kemit) which means black.

Interestingly, Diop proceeds to show how this curse is conveniently put in the mouth of God in Jewish scripture and the Hamitic branch refers to the persecuted negroid people. He also points out, however, that when the European wants to explain the ancient Egyptian civilization, Ham becomes whitened (as eastern and western Hamites) and is used officially to explain the civilization in Egypt. In essence, then, this version and arrangement of the story, attributes black civilization to white Hamites! This is referred to as the Hamitic Hypothesis.

Thus, one vision floating around in the European psyche, along with Santa Claus, sugar plums, and the white infant Jesus, is the imagery of persecuted Jews building the magnificent edifices of Egypt. Pharaohs are conjured up who are mentally portrayed as barbaric, while thousands maybe millions of persecuted people, among whom surely were the Jews, are envisioned as hoisting and hauling huge rocks to build the pyramids (which of course) were long in existence before the Jew). Today there is accumulating evidence that such industry among "slaves" never occurred, especially in building the pyramids.

A recent technical study of the pyramids seems to uncover and disclose a most interesting fact about the pyramid structure which would defy and eliminate the prevailing theory that thousands of enslaved men carried rock to build these ancient skyscrapers.

Dr. Joseph Davidovits, along with his assistant, Marge Morris, has presented an entirely differing picture of how the pyramids were constructed. Dr. Davidovits is a scientist specializing in low-temperature mineral synthesis. In the 1970's he found Cordi (Coordination and Development of Innovation), a research company, and the Geopolymer Institute, in France. He is recognized as founding a "new" branch of chemistry that he named " geopolymerization."

But Davidovits, unlike other recent "discoverers" (such as Columbus, Euclid, Hippocrates) gives credit to the ancients whom he now believes already had such knowledge and were using it. In essence, he is saying in his book, *The Pyramids,* that the builders of the pyramids were knowledgeable of geopolymers, that is, they knew how to make synthetic building materials such as cements and enamels. Here is Davidovits presenting his evidence:

The Great Pyramids reflect a technology of the ancient world that yields a sophisticated product or result but has no relationship to what we think of today as advanced or high technology. To visit the Pyramid Age would be to enter a world in which our objective, secular view of science does not exist. Anciently, in Egypt, science and religion were part of one body of knowledge, and the priests were responsible for fostering and preserving the knowledge.[43]

He goes on to mention the gods associated w particular arts and sciences, like Ptah, the god of craftsman, and Khnum, the Divine Potter."...It was Khnum whom the technology in question was attributed. Thc was the god of writing, and the knowledge of Khnum v written in the book of Thoth." These gods were simply emanations or expressions of the One god, one knowledge.

The science most germane to pyramid construction, says Davidovits, is overlooked today:

The mystery science has nothing to do with the classical physics of electricity, heat, optics, or mechanics, or anything in common with Quantum physics —atomic, nuclear, or sol id state. The science that made pyramids possible was chemistry and or, more precisely, its forerunner, alchemy.[44]

Davidovits gives credit to the origin of the word chemistry, presents impressive evidence of how knowledgeable the ancient Egyptians were of combining minerals to produce things like enamel or cement. Stones were seen as possessing sacred, eternal qualities, and were used exclusively in religious monuments. Stones were symbolic of the sacred realm. Says Davidovits:

The priest of Khnum had long been adept at the art of making extraordinary cements. Cement found in various parts of the courses of the Great Pyramid is about 4500 years old, yet it is still in good condition.[45]

Thus, his thesis:

> *If the ancient Egyptians had the ability to produce exceptionally high-quality cement, what prevented them from adding fossil shells to their cement to produce high-quality limestone concrete? The answer is that nothing prevented them. I will demonstrate that the pyramid blocks are not natural stone; the blocks are actually exceptionally high-quality limestone concrete--synthetic stone--cast directly in place. The blocks consist of about ninety to ninety-five percent cement. They are imitations of natural limestone, made in the age-old religious tradition of alchemical stonemaking. No stone cutting or heavy hauling or hoisting was ever required for pyramid construction.*[46]

I cannot say if Davidovits' construction thesis is accurate or not since I am not a geopolymer scientist nor expert on pyramidical construction. But his cultural and historical evidence, the context of the theory, is presented in accuracy. He tells the truth about ancient Egyptian high technology which was really their chemical acumen. He places his physical evidence correctly in the religious tradition of ancient Kemet. If he is correct, this is strong evidence that there was no need for oppressive and enslaving pharoahs to exploit the labor of thousands or millions of men to haul and hoist rocks. They were master craftsmen; master stonemasons (which knowledge the Europeans stole and hid in the mysteries and secrets of freemasonry).

Davidovits' information reveals that the ancient Egyptians were a knowledgeable people who had possession of geopolymerization and their extraordinary abilities as stonemasons rested not in brawn (theirs or that of slaves) but brain: the knowledge of chemistry.

There was a need, therefore, for European historian scholars to connect Jesus to "Jews" as a separate persecuted people not kin to the Africans but only enslaved by their pharoahs (who would be lightened in color as well through the process of writing history). Jesus would then be associated with the light skinned Jews of later times, European derived, rather than the original dark skinned Hebrews.

In an interview conducted by Legrand H. Clegg II for *Sepia* magazine in 1980, Professor Locksley Geoghagen is asked extensively about Jesus as a black man. Geoghagen establishes Jesus' identity as one of the world's sixteen crucified saviors, and his participation in the spiritual group called Essenes. According to Geoghagen, Essene doctrine is directly traceable to its African-Egyptian roots. Not only does he place early Christianity in the womb of ancient Egyptian religious tradition, but he also provides extensive documentation of the black paintings and statues of Jesus and his mother which proliferated in early Christian times and were whitened as the Roman Church took precedence and engaged artists like Michelangelo to paint European versions.[47]

Cheikh Anta Diop has provided voluminous material on the origins of African, Arab and Jew. The "Semetic" arises in the 4th millenia B.C. as a crossbreeding between black inhabitants of the holy land and white northern invaders.[48] In other words, Jesus' direct ancestors were *in* the holy land long before there was " Jew," and his lineage predates the "semetic" presence.

The truth about Jesus and the truth about ancient Egypt as well as early Christianity have all been concealed, and in the Western world they are locked in the coded secrecy of freemasonry.

FREEMASONRY

Freemasonry is the knowledge, study and practice of various degrees of the ancient Egyptian mystery religion. Its symbols are embedded in the implements and tools of ancient stonemasonry. The rituals and body of knowledge are today concealed and practiced in lodges and halls hidden from the common man, the masses of people.

While there has been this longstanding cover-up and continuous disinformation surrounding ancient Egypt, origins of man, and Jesus the Christ, to the point that European history yields very little direct connection to the ancient origin point in any true way, still it cannot be overlooked that there were those who knew, who perpetrated the lie. In order for the European to take the knowledge out of Egypt and keep it, it had to be hidden and preserved in a way that the people would not know in general. Those approved and selected of "belonging" to such societies would have access, but not the "common run of man."

It is said in most encyclopedia that freemasonry sprang up in Europe in the 1700's. The actual source of its knowledge is never fully expounded upon. But masons themselves recognize the source.

They know it is traced to ancient Africa (Kemet). A mason, Norman F. de Clifford wrote almost a century ago:

Practical, operative masonry was thoroughly comprehended (before the building of the temple of Ornan, the Jebusite) as evidenced by those stupendous and magnificent temples that existed in the land of old Khemi, upon the banks of the Nile, ages before David, King of Israel, bought the land from Ornan whereon to erect a temple to the most High God in which to practice the esoteric teachings handed down to us from one generation to another.[49]

The 1700 date becomes clear when considered in th context of all that went before. The King James Version (the Bible in 1611, the Ussher calendar as late as 1700, an slavery in full force. By this time the cover-up had bee completed, the connection to ancient Africa total severed, and white Christianity was forging the founding and settlement of America through a thriving slave traffic and plantation culture.

It is to be noted that early so-called founding fathers were masons: George Washington, John Hancoc Benjamin Franklin. In most biographies of Franklin the may be mention of his joining the lodge but very little else concerning his being a mason. Franklin was also companion of France's Count Volney who as a scholar al world traveler had seen and recorded in his writings the evidence of ancient African civilization.[50] Even so, Frank! did not publicize this knowledge, nor did any of the other early masons who were engaged in building America I the labor of slaves. But they used the knowledge. Says Tony Browder:

It is no accident that the so-called Founding Fathers sough to recreate, here in America, the same energies which guided and directed our ancestors in ancient Egypt. They utilized African architecture, science and symbolism and removed the African signature. Only a properly trained eye is capable of seeing the truth.

Further attempts to utilize the knowledge of the Africans can be found in the development of Masonry in the early foundation of the country. The Masons patterned themselves after the so-called mystery schools of Ancient Africa. Many of the Founding Fathers were Masons, as were all of the generals who fought in the Revolutionary War. George Washington insisted that only his Masonic brothers would command his troops.[51]

Browder continues to establish the links between Masonry and ancient Egypt, as well as the Declaration of Independence and the Constitution.

Is it any surprise today that America's " business" is conducted in similar "lodge-like" atmospheres? High level government officials and foreign dignitaries meet in clandestine places like "the Grove" in California, where they wine and dine each other calculating out the agenda for European (American) power. The Trilateral Commission, with its wealthy foundation in David Rockefeller, and the Council on Foreign Relations, appear to be public international groupings working towards "better relations." But in fact they are arenas for the great European and North American powers to negotiate a future while controlling the economies of the so-called "developing" Third World. Larry Abraham includes in his book *Call It Conspiracy* a chart showing the detailed membership of the C.F.R./Trilateral Commission connection. While I would question Abraham's accuracy in identifying the "enemy" (he seems to see a communist "take-over" rather than the last efforts on the part of a dying 6,000 year long rule of white supremacy to hang on) he does provide some valuable research materials. There is a quote on that chart which is appropriate here:

The Trilateral Commission doesn't secretly run the world. The Council on Foreign Relations does that. (said by Winston Lord, C.F.R. "W" Magazine, Aug. 4-11, 1978. Fairchild Publications, 7 E 12th, N.Y. 10002). [52]

While Abraham may feel more comfortable with white nationalist hard core Americans than being quoted in this book, his research is worth looking at. It shows the methodology of the white supremacist mind seeking to maintain and secure economic and political rule over the world.

Caucasians need to wake up to the cover-ups. The only way to do this is to set about unfolding, tearing back the layers of false history (cover up) and coming face to face with the truth. Everyday white men and women in America go about their business in a trusting, vacuous, and robotic way seeming to believe their best interests are always in the calculations of white leaders. Having fallen victim to white supremacy and believing that "foreign" elements are always the source of economic and social troubles, they are blind to the tactics of the deceiver who rules everything from secret inner circles and out of the scope of a media which claims to report it all. The unthinking white man and woman will go to war with Blacks, Latinos and Native Americans on local and regional territories because they really believe their lives are at risk due to them rather than the governmental and economic powers behind the scenes which maneuver all the "ethnic groups" to be at odds in order to secure power and wealth to remain in the hands of a few. The white man and woman need to break out of the trapped history syndrome. The hippies tried in the 60'5 and 70's and were squelched and neutralized along with the Black Power Movement. I am not sure there is time for another chance, but this book is an effort to count on that one last chance.

THE MEANING OF HISTORY FOR WHITE AMERICANS

In a profound article entitled "Listen to the Blood: the Meaning of Black History," historian Lerone Bennett, Jr. says: "The history of African Americans is, among other things, the history of a quest for meaning."[53] And this quest, says Bennett, unfolds within the context of knowing that this history is *real* (real, like getting arrested for riding through a white neighborhood, or your ancestor getting lynched, or receiving the blow of a billy club by some white officer in a demonstration of white power as you protest some form of injustice). Says Bennett, "We are by definition outsiders in the western world." He further concludes that black people have a mission, a world historical mission by virtue of their historical situation. Bennett pleads for a comprehension of history as it becomes a tool, a strategy, a life endeavor intimately linked with the struggle for liberation. "The history men and women make is a function of the meaning they give history. For it is from their practical philosophies, it is from the frames of reference they use to judge events and leaders and movements, that they get their level of hope and challenge."

I don't think it can be said that the history of European (white) Americans is a quest for meaning. It may be for some individual Caucasians, but as a nation, a collective psychology, white American history is not a quest, but a statement. It is the proclamation of a defined destiny, rooted in and propelled by a false consciousness. This consciousness operates from a posture of *ordainment.* That is, just as Blacks in America have operated from a posture of hope and struggle by virtue of seeing meaning and mission in their history, the Whites, on the other hand, have conducted themselves as the ordained, the chosen and superior people whose commission (not mission) has been to build "greatness" (in keeping with the inflated ego of a supremacist posture).

For the Black oppressed peoples, history instructs; it validates their sense of right and wrong; confirms their actions as being appropriate and morally correct in countering the actions of others as they oppress, torture, harm, and afflict black flesh and feeling.

But for the white oppressor, history does not instruct, it echoes and mirrors the narcissistic sense of greatness; it registers events and then leaves them there, completed, ended, dead. History therefore does not become instrumental in finding meaning or suggesting mission; it becomes an "annal" of doing, which somehow has nothing to do with personal conscience nor conduct in the present. History then, is taught as a track record of great feats and achievements, rather than as a path of human attempts and failures, which are subject to accountability and conscientious criticism.

The writing of white history then becomes a process of concealment, amelioration, and palatable wording. For example, Morris and Commager in the *Encyclopedia of American History,* describe slavery as follows:

1619, Aug. First Negroes (20) imported into Va. as bound servants. (the authors' emphasis)
1691-90. Importations of African Negroes continued on a moderate scale (only 3,000 Negroes estimated in Va., 1681) as white servants continued to perform bulk of farm labor.

By the use of words "moderate" and "only" and the juxtaposition of the slave with white servants, the authors somehow seem to lessen the impact of chattel slavery. They view it as a "form of labor." Their 1619 date is also Incorrect, though it be the one commonly used in American history. Slaves were brought at an earlier time, in the area of 1555.

In their account of John Brown's raid, Morris and I Comager saw fit to include:

"No slaves came to the aid of the attackers. "This comment implies enslaved Blacks were not in the least sympathetic to the effort to release them from slavery.

Imperialism of course is called "territorial expansion " and the authors move into a discussion of the assault on the Native American (Indian) by building a case that they (Indians) were warring among themselves, and later "becoming blended with European war practices." White aggression is called "white penetration." And the Five Civilized Nations were said to be "moved over the Trail of Tears" to Indian territory (Oklahoma). "Moved over" covers up the forced relocation which resulted in genocidal elimination of thousands of the natives. The Seminoles, they say, were "all but exterminated," somehow leaving the reader with the notion that they {the Seminoles) managed to survive and overcome while failing to dwell on the slaughter that did occur in the Seminole Wars. Osceola, the great Seminole warrior, is not even mentioned in the entire encyclopedia.

This adjustment of history to facilitate the psyche of white supremacy leads to ultimate illusion and totally false consciousness. That is why the white students I encounter will almost automatically move into defensive attitudes and will usually counter real history (as presented from the Black {African} side, the Native American side, the Chicano side, etc.) with a mental move of denial and justification of the common understanding that prevails in white history. Say for example I elaborate on how Native Americans were forced to relocate off their land, some white student may come back with: "But that's how progress is. And they weren't doing anything themselves to progress on the land." Or I might focus on how traditional ways of life were totally disrupted and most often eradicated, and the white students (and sometimes white thinking black students} might respond with: "But they're better off technologically by assimilating into mainstream America. You can't hold back progress." I might add, however, in recent classes I have found far more astonishment and shock at the deeds of the American government and industry towards Native Americans among the white students. Perhaps this generation will be the one to embrace the historical endeavor. However, when I suggest that the "drug epidemic" is really one aspect of the government's and ruling white circle's genocidal plan towards black male youth in particular, the students cannot fathom that and cry "paranoia."

Unlike Black history, white history is not real; because of I the initial moments of cover up, concealment, and ultimately prevarication, white history simply escapes the attachment of self to reality via historical analysis and narration. It links the individual to interpretations of past and present that somehow leave out the meaning for all involved. There is no meaning other than that superimposed upon the "events" which basically pose no human dilemma for the individual white American. And if meaning is superimposed on events, like the morally inflated pictures of "founding fathers" and the "heroic" immigrations of European ancestors, the white student, when confronted with the actual conditions of these events, can hardly bear to view them from such "negative" perspectives. For, the "past" has been a list of meritorious achievements, rather than a record of terroristic acts.

While Blacks were orally remonstrating their offspring to *never* forget Emmit Till for example, Whites were busy trying to soften the atrocity of the event, just as today the alleged rape and heinous assault on Tawana Brawley is being "written " into history in a maze of confusion, disinformation, and coverup surrounding her credibility and the actual events.[54]

In short, then, Black history involves remembrance, reflection, and human personal meaning. White history involves concealment, omission, and human personal indifference. Because of this inability to seek the meaning in history, Whites fail to make the necessary linkages between events. For example, they don't seem to see connections between American industry and world hunger; or military objectives and "foreign uprisings."

And possibly more tragic is the fact that white history gives no indication nor impulse towards mission. What mission is implied in a history that leaves a trail of violent destruction no matter how palatably worded? When the rewritten history is presented, "cleaned u p, " for its readers, what is left to inspire meaning and mission? When the characters in the historical narrative are presented only from a posture of ordainment, rather than a critical light, they are not real. They lack human dilemma; possibility of error.

If there is ever to be any sense of justice and equity within the white society, there first of all has to be the commitment to know the truth of self. Who is self? Self is one's own self plus the extension of self by virtue of ancestry and lineage. Self knowledge translates into knowledge of all that has occurred and existed to bring me (self) to this place and this time.

For Caucasians in America this excavation into the lives and deeds of foreparents, into the acts and motives of historical person-ages, can be painful and overwhelming. But it has to be done in order for the white-wash to wear off and the utter truth of darkness to emerge to purge the consciousness of false security, erroneous detail, and illusions of greatness and superiority. Once this is achieved by individual white Americans, their historians can no longer be allowed to misrepresent any of the past. The reason white Americans need to be immersed in Black history is not to learn a few facts about black contributions to the culture of America, but to see, for the first time most likely, the truth; to descend into the reality of what actually hap-pened.

Most students, most people in white America, avoid this descent into history (which is really a way to ascend to liberation). I did once have a Jewish student who was appalled at the realization that Ancient Egyptians were black. She told me she felt cheated and that a "big number" had been done on her. But she was strong enough to at least recognize it. Once white people realize Black history is their key to self liberation and the way to avoid white supremacy thinking, they will hopefully embrace the historical endeavor with great fervor. It is scandalous that even up to the present time, there are still efforts to separate Egypt from black Africa. Two incidents come to mind.

One was a story carried in the Baltimore *Afro-American* (July 14, 1987 issue). Apparently a group of black youth in Baltimore were planning a city funded trip to Egypt. The youth, in their own news-paper called *"City Scoop"*, referred to Cairo, Egypt, as part of Africa, and were censored for it. A Ms. Redmond who was associated with the trip and youth is reported as saying: "In particular, most members (of the mayor's office) resented the fact that the kids referred to their destination, Cairo, Egypt, as part of Africa. As a result the city did not provide funding for the students' trip."

The other incident surrounded a statement by the cultural attache at the Egyptian Embassy in Washington, Mr. Abdel-Latif Aboul-Ela. Mr. Aboul-Ela claimed that Egyptians are not related to the original "black Africans." His remarks were published in the *Washington Post,* March 23, 1989.[55] White supremacy has overtaken even non-European minds.

It is time for the white man and woman in America to look closely at the teachings of the Honorable Elijah Muhammad, in order to get some idea of their own nature and psyche. The denial and fear of truth will only bring about destruction much more quickly. For some it is possible to extricate themselves from the diabolical scheme of white supremacy. W.E.B. DuBois, having labored all of his life against the obstacles presented by a white supremacist regime (whether in his childhood experiences or the halls of so-called high-er learning) put the case quite well for white Americans:

Indeed, the greatest and most immediate danger to white culture, perhaps least sensed, is its fear of the truth, its childish belief in the effi-cacy of lies as a method of human uplift.[56]

And, in accordance, the meaning of black history becomes all too significant for white culture and history, in DuBois' suggestion that the black world "must be seen as existing not simply for itself but as a group whose insistent cry may yet become the warning which awakens the world to its truer self and its wider destiny."

NOTES

(Chapter 1)

1.) James Baldwin and Margaret Mead, A *Rap on Race* (N. Y. : Lippincott, 1971), p. 69.

2.) James Baldwin, *The fire Next Time* (N. Y.: Dial Press, 1963), p. 22.

3.) Elijah Muhammad, *Message to the Blackman in America* (Philadelphia: Hakim's Pub., 1965), p. 53.

4.) *Ibid.*

5.) *Ibid.*, p. 42.

6.) *Ibid.*, p. 88.

7.) L. S. B. Leakey, *The Progress and Evolution* of *Man in Africa* (London: Oxford University Press, 1961)., pp.1;3.

8.) Mark Stoneking and Rebecca L. Cann, " African Origin of Human Mitochondrial DNA," Final Draft for the Cambridge Symposium: The Origins and Dispersal of Modern Humans: Behavioral Biological Perspectives, July 8, 1987. Also see A. C. Wilson, M. Stoneking, R. L. Cann, E. M. Prager, S. D. Ferris, L. A. Wischnik, and R. G. Higuchi, "Mitochondrial Clans and the Age of Our Common Mother," in *Human Genetics*, ed. by F.Vogel and K. Sperling (Berlin-Heidelberg: Springer-Verlag, 1987). See also Maitland A. Edey and Donald C. Johanson, *Blue- prints: Solving the Mystery* of *Evolution* (Boston: Little Brown and Company, 1989). Cheikh Anta Diop, " Africa: Cradle of Humanity," in *Nile Valley Civilizations* (Proceedings of the Nile Valley Conference, Atlanta, Sept. 26-30, 1984 -Morehouse College Edtion, Journal of African Civilizations Ltd., Inc.,edited by Ivan Van Sertima, 1985).

9.) Michael Bradley, *The Iceman Inheritance: Prehistoric Sources* of *Western Man's Racism, Sexism and Aggression* (N. Y. : The African Islamic Mission Publications -Collectors Edtion of 1978 original)

10.) See the Proceedings of the Annual Melanin Conferece,Washington 1988-1989, Video-taped. Also see Anthony T. Browder, *From the Browder File* (Washington, D.

C.: Institute of Karmic Guidance, 1989), pp. 91-95. Frances Cress Welsing, *Cress Theory* of *Color confrontation* (wash ing- ton DC.: C-R Pub., 1970. Carol Barnes, *Melanin: The Chemical Key* to *Black Greatness* (Houston: Black Greatness Series, 1988).

11.) Ashley Montague, *Science and Creationism* (Oxford U. Press, 1984).

12.) See James Ussher, *The Annals* of *the Old and New Testament, with the Synchronifimus* of *Heathen Story* to *the Destruction* of *Jerusalem by the Romans* (London: Printed by E. Tyler, for J. Clark at the Sign of the Ship in St. Paul's Churchyard and for G. Bidell, at the Middle- Temple Gate in Fleet St. MDC LVIII 1658. Ussher writes: "In the Beginning God created Heaven and Earth (Gen. 1, v. 1) which beginning of time, according to our chronologue, fell upon the entrance of the night, preceding the 23rd day of October in the Julian Calendar, 710." (4004 B.C .in his, Ussher's, calendar). Also see James A. Carr, *The Life and Times* of *James Ussher, Archbishop* of *Armagh* (London: Wells Gardner, Darton & co., 1895). C. R. Elrington and J. H. Todd, eds., *The Works of James Ussher,* 17 volumes, Reprint of 1864 (AMS Press). In my father's family bible, Ussher's calendar still was included as late as 1866, the date of its publication by the American Bible Society, N. V. The calendar appears in the center of the page running with the text. It says, "year before the common *year* of Christ, 4004 --Julian period, 0710 --cycle of the sun, 0010 --Dominical Letter, B. Cycle of the moon, 007 -- Indiction 0005 --Creation from Tisri, 0001.

13.) *See* W. E. B. DuBois' *The Suppression of the African Slave Trade* (N. V.: Russel & Russell, 1965) Orig. pub. in 1898.

14.) See Philip Gosse's *Hawkin's Scourge of Spain,* 1930, and other biographies.

15.) Herodotus, *History,* Book 11, 16. See English translation *The History of Herodotus,* tr. by G. Rawlinson.

16.) See George G. M. James, *Stolen Legacy* (San Francisco: Julian Richardson, 1976) .

17.) Kenneth Scott Latourette, A *History of Christianity* (N. V. : Harper & Row, 1953), p. 153. Also see H. M. Gwatkin,

Studies of A ria nism,1882 or 1900.

18.) Rev. Charles Francis Potter, *The Lost Years of Jesus Revealed* (N. V.: Fawcett Gold Medal Books, 1962). p. 117.

19.) Gwatkin, *op. cit.*

20.) *Glanville Downey, Ancient Antioch* (Princeton University Press, 1963), pp. 153-55.

21.) Interview with Dr. Charles Finch, conducted by Listervelt Middleton, South Carolina Educational Television, "For the People Program", 1990.

22.) Interview with Professor Locksley D. M. Geoghagen, by Leland CIegg II. *Sepia* Magazine, Sept.-Oct., 1980. "Was Jesus Christ Black?"

23.) Chancellor Williams, *The Destruction of Black Civilization* (Chicago: Third World Press, 1987), p. 135 and Chapter VI.

24.) Potter, *op. cit.* I p. 39.

25.) *Ibid.,*

26.) Williams, *op. cit.*, p. 37.

27.) James, *op. cit.*, p. 5; p. 154.

28.) Robin Lane Fox, *Pagans and Christians* (N. V .: Alfred A. Knopf., 1987), p. 681.
Introduction by John Henrik Clarke, to *The Cultural Unity of Black Africa*, by Cheikh Anta Diop (Chicago: Third World Press, 1990- first pub. in 1978).

29.) Introductionby John Henrik Clarke, to *The Cultural Unity of Black Africa*, by Cheikh Anta Diop (Chicago: Third World Press, 1990-first pub. in 1978).

30.) *Encyclopedia Britannica,* Iconoclasm; Iconoclastic Controversy.

31.) *Ibid*

32.) *See* 1970 and early 1980 issues of A. M *Journal* (also Called *Muslim Journal* and *Bilalian News,* depending on year of publication)

33.) *See* Darwin's *Descent of Man* (1871) Also L S 8 Leakey, " Africa's Contribution to Human Evolution,H *The Progress and Evolution* of *Man in Africa* (London. Oxford University Press, 1961)

34.) Edward Luries, *LouiS Aggasiz: A Life* of *Science* (Chicago U of Chicago Press, 1960), *p* 257.

35.) Dorothy Sterling, ed, *We Are Your Sisters: Black Women in the Nineteenth Century* (N Y : Norton, 1985), p 18.

36.) Thomas H Huxley, *Man's Place in Nature* (Ann Arbor U of Michigan Press, 1959), p 19.

37.) *Ibid,* p 21.

38.) Cheikh Anta Diop, *The African Origln of Civilization: Myth or Reality* (Ed and tr by Mercer Cook) (Westport: Lawrence Hill & Co, 1974), p 5.

39.) *Ibid,* p. 6.

40.) *Ibid.,* p. 7. Diop also discusses the identity of the Jew in *The Cultural Unity of Black Africa, op.cit.,pp* 100-101.

41.) Yosef A A ben-Jochannan, *The African Called Rameses* II *("The Great")* Exhibition April 29, 1989, Dallas, Texas) p 58.

42.) *Ibid,* p 39.

43.) Joseph Davidovits and Margie Morris, *The Pyramids* An *Enigma Solved* (N Y.: Hippocrene Books, Inc, 1988), p 65.

44.) *Ibid,* p 66.

45.) *Ibid.,* p 68.

46.) *Ibid.*

47.) Geoghagen interview, *(Sepia), op. cit.*

48.) Diop, all works previously mentioned Also *see* his *Black Africa:The Economic and Cultural Basis* for *a Federated State* (tr by H Salemson, Westport. Lawrence Hill & Co, rev editon, 1987), Foreword.

49.) Norman F. de Clifford, *From Egypt, the Cradle* of *Ancient Masonry* (Philadlephia: Lincoln Pub Co, 1902), p. 17.

50.) Charles S Finch, III, HThe Black Roots of Egypt's Glory," *Washington Post,* October 11, 1987.

51.) Browder, *op cit,* pp 12-13.

52.) Larry Abraham, *Call it Conspiracy* (Seattle: Double A Pub, 1971), pp 83-85 *See* end charts.

53.) Lerone Bennett, Jr" "Listen to the Blood The Meaning of Black History," *Ebony* (Nov" 1985), p 184.

54.) See *Final Call,* June 16 and July 20, 1988, issues.

55.) *Baltimore Afro-American* (July 14, 1987) *Washington* Post (March 23, 1989) See Aziz Abdoela Batina's letter on Mr Aboul-Ela's statements in *Muslim* Journal (Many 13, 1989), p 23 Also see Yosef ben-Jochannan's *The African Called*

Rameses ("The Great") II already cited, which is largely a response to Aboul-Ela's statement.

56.) W E B DuBois, *Dusk* of *Dawn* (N Y: Harcourt, Brace & Son, 1940), p 172.

CHAPTER TWO

THE WHITE MAN

Not every Caucasian male need be a "white man." But every Caucasian male in America inherits the legacy of the white man, and most embrace this bequeathal in the absence of godly parentage. White becomes a state of mind.

As mentioned earlier, according to Elijah Muhammad and the teachings passed on to him, the Caucasians came about through the genetic manipulations (grafting) of one of the original people, Yakub. Yakub was said to be born around 6,600 years ago, 20 miles from Mecca, that is about 4,000 B.C., although the scientist of ancient times are said to have known of him and his rule to come, some 15,000 years ago.

This "new made-man" was made to be against the righteous rule of the Almighty God of the universe, according to these teachings, and would rule the world for approximately 6,000 years, while the Black descendants of the Original People were "asleep," that is, mentally dead to their own righteous nature and anesthetized, you could say, and immobilized by the teachings of westernized white Christianity and the false image of a white Jesus, thus generating in them a time of self hatred. The chronology of the above fits the historical incidents discussed in Chapter One regarding the appearance of the European or white man around 4,000 B.C., his eviction from the ancient holy lands (Asia-Africa) and the emergence of white Christian rule.[1]

Whether one accepts this explanation of the white man's birth and rule, or prefers to believe the Caucasian simply emerged from having emigrated out of the original and of the Blacks and became caucasoid and depigmented through climate and terrain, the result is the same: the European or Aryan people became an errant people, who did not possess the original righteous way {though they knew of it and copied much of it, later to be codified in freemasonry), who lacked melanin and pigmentation of the skin, who apparently had no "dream-time" (that is, a creation story and genealogical memory via oral history), and who, according to the Messenger, Elijah Muhammad, had no sense of shame. Whatever the cause, these deficiencies seem to be uniquely interrelated, resulting in one and the same pathology: white supremacy and its character structure that came to be the mark of "mankind" (the imitation made white race).

In time, the European becomes "the white man" in a more political sense than just pigmentation. In fact, James Baldwin says very directly in *The Fire the Next Time* that "color is not a human or personal reality; it is a political reality."[2] This white man is a made man; or as Elijah Muhammad said, a kind of man--mankind--imitation. He is generated and sustained by grandiose imagery and false consciousness. His self reflection is inverted, so that he sees himself not in the image of true godliness, that is, human perfection, but in the illusions of godlike power, or as Eldridge Cleaver put it in *Soul On Ice*, back in the '60's during his revolutionary days: "the omnipotent administrator."[3]

In teaching college and university classes through the years, I have felt a sharp tinge of anxiety when facing young Caucasian men, knowing somehow I and they would eventually have to identify, analyze, and lay bare the truth of themselves to themselves. Any excursion into history, any discussion of current social affairs and political power, and any analysis of male/female behavior, would inevitably lead to the reality of white supremacy and the attributes commonly associated with this psychological construct: domination, oppression, arrogance, and unprincipled power. In these classes it is not uncommon for some of the Caucasian women to become totally outraged at the history of white supremacy. A few have even launched into intensive reading and research, allowing their entire sensitivity to be immersed in the horrors of the past, having never had any idea that such terror had been the nature of the founding fathers or the founding of the society. But the young white men who are willing to allow themselves such immersion in the truth of their heritage are rare indeed. I can think of several outstanding examples.

UNCHECKED APPETITES
AND THE EMPIRE OF MATERIALISM

The main characteristic that stands out about the white man is his insatiable appetite for material accumulation and the haste with which he seeks it. Cheikh Anta Diop refers to this trait in his *Precolonial Africa*. In discussing the original concept of caste, based on division of labor, he contrasts the attitude of the European or Aryan :

> *Giving a divine character to property is an Aryan custom: in Rome, Greece, and India it led to the isolation from society of an entire category of individuals who had no family, had neither hearth nor home, and no right of ownership... It was through its concern with the ownership of material goods that the Aryan spirit or genius impressed its mold upon the caste system.* [4]

The white man works the opposite of nature. Rather than holding sacred that which is naturally endowed, he assigns power and reverence to his property, which becomes commercially and financially significant, rather I humanly and spiritually uplifting. It is noteworthy in recent newspaper reports of the United States sending troops to the Virgin Islands and the Guard to h Carolina in the aftermath of Hurricane Hugo, the House spokesman or the President himself consistently referred to the reason for doing so as protection of property and lives; always putting property. [5]

There has been no creature on the face of the earth who has demonstrated anti-natural behavior more than the white man. This anti-nature posture is what allows him to 'sue with unconscionable haste his hunger for power I possession. All through his history this man has done everything to upset and ruin the balance in nature, that harmony in natural law and the very order within human nature itself. He manages to do this through deception. 'en by strong appetites himself, he has an incredible ability to deceive and generate or create an appetite within his associates (so-called friends or enemies) which will eventually weaken and immobilize them, possibly destroying them, and the balance in which they might have once lived.

Elijah Muhammad says in *Message to the Blackman* that the white man (devil) was called Caucasian, and according to some Arab scholars, this means "one whose evil effect is not confined to one's self alone, but affects others." [6] In his narration of Yakub and his devils, they eventually were chased out of the ancient holy lands to the island of Pelan, and he tells how Mr. Yakub taught his followers to deceive the righteous people (a pattern still used effectively in the U.S. today and elsewhere, the F.B.I. being one of the main agents of such craft):

...When you go back to the holy Black nation, rent a room in their homes. Teach your wives to go out the next morning around the neighbors of the people. and tell that you heard her talking about them last night. When you have gotten them fighting and killing each other. then ask them to let you help settle their disputes. and restore peace among them. If they agree. then you will be able to rule them both. [7]

On a global basis, this tactic occurs everyday, right today, most likely involving some people whose intentions are good, but the motives behind the overall larger plan of which they may not even be aware of, are usually devious and designed to result in control of a nation and its economy. Example: Former President Jimmy Carter being used on a "mediation" mission for Ethiopia. The Ethiopian Mengistu government (not at all favored by the U.S. government) is supposedly at "civil war" with its Eritrean population in the north. The u.s. government, whose ambassador was ousted in 1980, now seizes an opportunity to "intervene" in the so-called civil war (who fuels the fires of Eritrean discontent?) and "mediate" the dispute. Such mediation characteristically requires "evidence of shifts by the Ethiopian government in several key areas...and major economic reforms that could make U.S. aid effective." [8]

Go back to Elijah Muhammad's description of this devil tactic: "when you have gotten them fighting and killing each other, then ask them to let you help settle their disputes, and restore peace among them. If they agree, then you will be able to rule them both." One also is led to wonder about the "accidental" death of Rep. Mickey Leland, reportedly on good relations with Ethiopian head of state, Mengistu. Was his death the necessary "incident" for the u.s. to enter into the country's affairs under the mask of seeking cooperation? From the

Washington Post:

> *The "spirit of cooperation" shown by Ethiopia in the search for Rep. Mickey Leland (D-Tex) and his companions may presage an improvement in the rocky relationship between the United States and that important African country, the State Department said yesterday.*[9]

Using tactics of deception and feigned friendliness, the white man can move in among people and generate appetites for things which will bring him (the white man) profit. He can generate or activate these appetites among people of his own kind as well as among people of other races or ethnic heritage. There is no better place that we can see this ability to generate some appetite in another in order to trick and rob him than in the early industrial and economic history of this country. I am referring to the rum-for-slaves trafficking (is it anything new that today it is the same tactic, but different products: arms-for-drugs).

Europeans for a long time indulged in alcoholic beverages, especially the distilled kind. Original and indigenous peoples did not indulge, although there was knowledge to be sure of fermentation which resulted in natural wines and beverages. When the New England industrialists in the 1700's found out that their surplus of inferior salt fish could be useful to the West Indies plantation owners who would feed them to the slaves, these industrialists entered into one of the most degrading trade agreements ever witnessed. The New England industrialists took a by-product surplus off the West Indies plantation owners' hands; molasses. And these European West Indies plantation owners took a large supply of cheap salt fish off the New England market. The molasses was eventually made into rum by the New England industrial capitalists. Writing in 1918, J.H. Moore says:

> *A quantity of molasses made an equal quantity of rum, and a gallon of rum costing little more than sixpence to produce was worth 1,000 per cent more in Africa, where almost all the New England rum was sent.*[10]

The African did not have an appetite for rum until the European introduced it, promoted it, and trafficked in it. This New England entrepreneur was even more clever, however, in his manipulation of appetite and profit:. the cask of rum, Moore tells us, could be left out on the deck in the blazing sun, which would raise the proof or "make the rum more fiery in its effects," and " a watering process whereby the rum was increased by a third of its bulk, could be carried out without detection."[11]

So this early American—the white man—engaged in a vicious cycle of appetite profiteering. He generated two fundamental appetites that would remain in the structure of American society: the appetite for alcohol and that for slaves (or cheap exploited servile labor in later years). He methodically sold his fish to West Indian (European) plantationers for their molasses; distilled the molasses into rum; traded the rum in Africa for gold dust and slaves, and sold the slaves back on this side of the Atlantic, usually in the South, and West Indies.

Someone recently argued with me that "the North" never depended on slavery to build its part of the nation, but the early foundations of the northeast industrial sector of America were indeed solidly planted in the African slave trade. Moore points out that Peter Faneuil, one of these wealthy capitalists in Boston, furnished the capital for the slave trade. His ships carried rum distilled from the West Indies molasses, then was exchanged for gold dust and slaves. Faneuil Hall in Boston, often referred to as "the cradle of liberty" was thus built on this unsavory trade, and a saying about Faneuil Hall came from this: "The cradle of liberty rocks on the bones of the middle passage."[12]

We should also recognize that during the same years of this Triangular Trade, the white man was introducing alcohol to the Native Americans in order to deceive and weaken them to get what they wanted from them, namely land.

According to the Dictionary of American History, this "triangular trade" started in New England around 1621 and "maintained the prosperity of the northern colonies through the 18th Century." W.E.B. DuBois points out that the rum distillery industry indicates to some extent the activity of New England in the slave trade.[13]

Clifford Alderman gives a detailed account of how the white man used rum to not only trade in flesh, but used it to weaken the bargaining powers of the African collaborators who were seduced into the slave traffic. He tells how the slavers would "dash" (bestow gifts upon) the African collaborators with much rum, getting them intoxicated, while they themselves would weaken their own drinks with water so as to remain sober.[14]

It should be noted that the F.B.I. in particular and the government in general continued to utilize this tactic of "dashing," that is, offering lavish gifts of salary, lodging, expenses, clothing and "protection" and even drugs-- to 20th Century collaborators (infiltrators) on their clandestine operations aimed at the Black Panthers and the American Indian Movement as well as other similar groups in the 1960's.[15]

Alderman also relates how some "witchdoctors" could be seduced into securing slaves, first by "dashing" them with rum (the pure stuff), then the "witchdoctors" would assemble the people and trick them by accusing them of black magic and then take them away from the village to the slave fort or factory where they would be held and taken onto boats for delivery in the Americas.

The European was clever (and deceitful) enough to water down the hogsheads of rum that had been traded for slaves and left with the African collaborators. So the collaborators weren't even getting what they paid for in human flesh.

W.E.B. DuBois demonstrates clearly in his *Suppression of the African Slave Trade* how New England not only thrived on this triangular trade but how it continued to support the slave trade. The Northeast colonies didn't so much import the slaves for use in the North, but served as carrier and middle-men by delivering the slave cargoes to southern colonies and the West Indies. From 1700, Rhode Island became the greatest slave trader in America. She served as a clearinghouse for the trade of other colonies. More than thirty distilleries were running, and one hundred fifty vessels in the slave trade. In Newport alone twenty-two distilleries ran at one time. Massachusetts distilled 15,000 hogshead of molasses.[16]

This characteristic of generating appetitive addictions in a population and then capitalizing on them seems to be the nature of the white man. While reading James Granger's account of Adam (that is, the white man or European) and his trajectory through time and human civilization, I ran across his citing the comments of T. Obinkaram Echewa, a Nigerian writing about America. Echewa said: "The' American way of life' is not founded on the interplay of human virtues supporting and encouraging one another, but rather on competing human appetites keeping one another in check." [17]

I would like to add to this that after the white man activates or generates the appetite, he feeds it to the point of saturation and beyond. The beyond is seen in the new combinations of drugs, once the older ones become familiar, used, and over-used, like cocaine, which then became crack cocaine; or marijuana gets mixed with chemicals. After total saturation and especially if people begin to tire of the addiction and want out, then the same suppliers are on hand with a counter-capitalizing effort which downplays the addiction (and also penalizes it such as in public drunkenness, driving while intoxicated, making some substances illegal, etc.), and then brings out products to "treat" or "get rid" of the addiction such as near beers, nicotine free cigarettes, caffeine free coffee, artificial salt and sugar substitutes, and treatment drugs like methadone and weight loss pills.

The saga of the tobacco industry is a perfect example of this appetitive profiteering. Now that cigarette smoking is perceived here in the States as a negative activity (due to health hazards and unattractiveness) the tobacco industrial capitalists create less tar cigarettes and substitutes, not to mention, gimmicks and programs designed to cure the addiction. In true characteristic form and neo-colonialistic thinking, the industrialists move to promote the product and the appetite outside the country, and out of sight of the American public who are currently besieged with governmental and corporate agencies demanding smoke-free work places and public restraint. These same tobacco industrialists, who are fast trying to move their investments and capital into other industries, mostly food products, are also quietly promoting and pushing cigarettes in Third World nations. Dr. Judith MacKay, former director of the Hong Kong Council on Smoking and Health, and a member of the World Health Organization's Expert Advisory Panel on Tobacco and Health, states in an October, 1988, article:

The major concern about tobacco use in the world today is the increase in developing countries. While tobacco markets are decreasing in the West at the rate of one percent per annum, smoking is increasing in developing countries at an average of two per cent per annum. In other words, for every smoker who quits in the United States or Europe, two people start smoking in a developing country. [18]

Just as the white man introduced rum into Africa, distilled alcohol in general to Native Americans, he unconscionably moves to generate the appetite for smoking in the countries of non-European people in the Third World. MacKay further notes that the Western (white) tobacco industry operates with a different standard in developing countries. In Asia, for example, cigarettes are sold in some countries without health warnings that would be compulsory now in the United States. Says MacKay :

A recent analysis conducted by the American Health Foundation reported that American cigarettes sold in the Philippines yielded significantly higher values of tar, nicotine, and carbon monoxide than exactly the same brands sold in the U.S. And promotional campaigns have especially targeted women. [19]

MacKay says that recently in Beijing a senior health officer likened the cigarette campaign to a new opium war. She also pointed out that a WHO group of experts reported that "whereas in most industrialized countries the smoking habit is decreasing and becoming socially less acceptable, in developing countries it is on the increase, fueled mainly by intensive and ruthless promotional campaigns on the part of the transnational tobacco countries." These transnational companies from industrialized western nations, primarily the U.S., are simply the modern form of white industrialists profiteering off an appetitive addiction that they fostered and continue to promote. The WHO article demonstrates clearly how these transnational tobacco companies care little for the health of Third World peoples, not to mention how this one addiction can further deplete the financial resources of already poor men and women struggling to survive.

The costs to the targeted countries (for promotion) far outweigh benefits. These costs are ultimately accumulated in medical and health care; social welfare due to premature death and disability; loss of land use that could have been used for food production rather than tobacco. Behind the scenes the giant tobacco industries here in the U.S. (part of the transnational network) are hurrying to move their capital into other products such as food items.

The international cocaine trafficking is simply a continuation of the white man's triangular kind of economic control via the profits from appetitive addiction combined with the desperate human conditions of non- white populations who need both the drug and its related "jobs" in order to endure the desperate situation of chronic poverty. While a large percentage of the Black population in the U.S. seems to accept with certainty that the recent crack addiction in America is hardly an accident, but a well-planned and specifically designed strategy for further immobilizing an otherwise potentially revolu- tionary population of young black men, thus the entire Black community of women and family, white Americans seem unable to grasp the historically well-founded basis for believing this "conspiracy." If they would but seek out the historical precedents, just as I have done in the preceding pages on a limited basis, they would clearly arrive at the conclusion that America has been involved in such control tactics via appetites and their ensuing addictions, since her very inception.

In his testimony at the Special Session of the Seventh World Tribunal on Reparations for African People in the u.s. held in St. Petersburg, Florida, November 12-13, 1988, Ajamu Mwafrika spoke on the guns for drugs operation, as revealed in the various informations coming out of the Iran-Contra hearings and other legal testimonies. The driving forces, according to Ajamu, behind bringing drugs back into the U.S., mostly cocaine, was the Reagan administration's objective of keeping the Contras armed when such assistance was outlawed by Congress between October 1984 and 1986. Ajamu says the scenario went as follows:

Plane loads of Columbian cocaine were flown to the farmland in northern Costa Rica owned by an American rancher named John Hull. John Hull has been identified as a CIA and National Security Council liaison to the Contra bases in Costa Rica on the southern front of the U.S. War against Nicaragua. Senator Kerry had these hearings that say Hull claimed in 1984 and 1985 he received $10,000 a month from the National Security Council. It doesn't say what for though. It just says he received it—$120,000 a year.

Also, the cocaine on these planes came from Pablo Escobar and Jorge Ochoa, two major Columbian cocaine producers and traffickers who dominated the Medellin Cartel which accounted for 80 percent of the cocaine that they say comes into the U.S. and we know that of that 80 percent, probably 95 percent ends up in the oppressed African community.[20]

Ajamu refers to this operation as a triangle. It is a triangle involving Miami to Costa Rica, Guatemala, and Honduras. He says the whole triangle began about 1982. The items traded (like rum and slaves) were guns and drugs. Arms could get into Contra forces, drugs could get into the u.s. Simple as that. Ajamu further testified:

In May of 1985 the chief of the U.S. Drug Enforcement Agency in San Jose, Costa Rica, told local journalists that certain groups under the pretense of running guns to the contra rebels are smuggling drugs into the U.S. [21]

Note that "crack" appeared in the U.S. (New York specifically) around 1985; in Black inner cities of course.

Why do white Americans find it hard to ask the question: where did the crack addiction come from? How was the appetite generated for it? Why did it appear first in Black inner cities (like heroin, cocaine in its first form, and all the other addictive drugs, especially alcohol with its numerous "outlets" on every corner and in every block)? These questions need to be addressed by white Americans, since most black people in America have already asked and answered the questions. There are strong precedents for this kind of calculated economic profiteering and control via appetitive addictions through American history.

There is no limit of course on what kinds of appetites can be activated in a population, and then what products will be promoted to satisfy these appetites. Since the industrial capitalists have never shown any kind of respect for natural boundaries that would provide some modicum of protection to human development, they can invent and promote just about any product, and unless people are aware -- "hip to" --of the plan, they will become willing recipients of some new "need" being answered. Take for example, the "boom car" craze.

The car has long been understood to be a necessity in the western psyche (which is promoted to other psyches across the world). But now that the appetite for the car has been well established so that families want two or three, and celebrities may accumulate 40 or 50, can there be any further capitalizing off its presence? To be sure. In this day and age of electronics and high tech, the car becomes a sound studio on wheels. And since drug dealing and using has also become a part of the American landscape, the two become interlocked —that is, they have an affinity for one another. That is not to say that every person with a boom car is into drugs or dealing, but it is to say that one installer commented in a *Washington Post* article, that car stereos have become as much a part of the area's drug culture as the gold chain and beeper.[22]

Note again, the white man {because the industrial capitalists of this society are white, with a few lower level executives and entrepreneurs showing up dark) always seem to target the oppressed, colonized and non-white populations for introducing new appetitive demands and items to satisfy the new sensation now awakened as a "need." It really is a strategy to tap two levels of appetite. Always within the oppressed and controlled (colonized) sectors of a population there is a basic need to be somebody, to be noticed, to be more important than the society seems to allow. This psychological and emotional need to be more than what is allowed in white America is strong in black youth. Couple this need with the familiar maturational appetitive needs of becoming men and women, of belonging to a social community, and the appetite profiteers have an extremely vulnerable and exploitable target population. The "boom car" answers this more inward need of self-recognition while also satisfying energetic needs surrounding the rites of sexual maturation, demonstrating manly power and intellectual acumen (as seen in the knowledge of this mechanical and technical paraphernalia).

A boom car may have as many as eight speakers inside. The sound is enough to rattle windows, shake the roof and drown out sirens. The whole electronic wonder is a gimmick for making money, using the needs already embedded in nature while creating new needs in people already saturated with addictions. Manufacturers and dealers of this equipment sponsor national competitions called "sound-offs." Like other addictions, however, they don't stay confined to one population, they become a part of the entire landscape at some point, though motives may vary for involvement. The young black male who might also be drawn into the drug scene is an apt target for the boom car. Drew Garland, an installer of this equipment, is reported as saying in the *Washington Post* article: " A lot of times when I'm finished and ask them if they want to hear it, they close all the doors and windows, stand outside and put their hand on the windshield to feel the vibrations...They want to be noticed."

By the same token, Kenneth Bullough of Laurel, Md., who won the top prize in the Car Audio Nationals in 1988, owns a carpet business and regards his interest in stereo equipment in the car as a hobby. He says he rarely plays it loud enough for others outside to hear.

Even so, the manufacturers and dealers have made their profit either way. For one it may satisfy a basic emotional need for popularity, being noticed, being somebody in a society that has essentially rendered him nobody; for another it can satisfy the less impending but most tempting need to excel in a skill, to simply do a job well. Call it a hobby.

Once again, those involved in this appetitive capitalization have ignored mother nature.* Hearing specialists have for some time warned about the effects of listening to extremely loud music over long periods of time (mostly those at rock concerts or people addicted to earphones). David Resnick, Director of Hearing and Speech Center at Washington Hospital Center was quoted as saying:

> *There are a lot of kids who expose themselves to hazardous noise, and whether it's a car stereo or a Walkman headset... the ear was not meant to withstand that over its lifetime.*[23]

The list of appetites could go on and on with an array of products that have been manufactured through the years to answer some basic appetite that either has always been there or is activated by those who would profit from others' needs. Even the appetites that seem to be outside the scope of natural need have some kinship with basic human needs that are not being answered or are misdirected. The sadism and masochism forms of sexual gratifications, now offered as "services" at sex clinics or "S&M" establishments are simply aberrations of the basic human need to satisfy sexual drives, and also emotional and spiritual ones. It is a perversion of a basic appetite into a "new need" or what could be called a secondary appetite or artificially produced appetite. Drugs fit the category, and all sorts of crazes and fads that suddenly appear and take over a population for a certain length of time, and then just as quickly disappear as a new product and fad form on the horizon.

At this point, I should mention if the reader objects to this

capitalization on human appetites as being called a white man's pathology. and cites the number of Blacks involved In promoting the items themselves, he or she should realize by now that "white" is no longer confined to skin but it is a state of mind. a worldview and axiology that can be adapted by anyone if they are far enough away from the roots of self and natural being to be so led.

Even coffee, a still thriving industry, but declining in appetitive "needs" because of the caffeine (cancer) scare, being once more specially promoted by advertising in 'w appealing forms. Reporting in the *Washington Times,* Susan Dillingham describes the saga of America's most popular beverage in the 1960's" (three-fourths of e population over age 16 drank it). It took second place the soft drink craze since 1985. Says Dillingham:

concerned about the trend, the industry is devising a variety new products and promotions designed to win over the soda-guzzling public.

The gimmicks generate "new appetites" like the cool coffee craze. Apparently indifferent to the dangers of caffeine, the Coffee Development Group, a U.S. marketing and promotional organization, funded by coffee producing nations, has moved to bring young people into he market. Says Dillingham:

to entice a younger crowd, the group is moving its promotional efforts into shopping malls. Coffee Rock Cafe, a tasting promotion, targeted at teens, got underway last nonth.[24]

From bizarre sex to drugs to boom cards, to gold to Uzi's and AK-47's, people are daily being enticed, seduced, addicted, and thus controlled by external commercializing forces that prevent the human nature to surface, grow and fulfill its own mission of self mastery.

Now we can better understand why the cover-ups continue to occur that were discussed in Chapter One. "Truth," said the master to his student, Grasshopper, in the old Kung-fu television series, "is that which binds the self to the self." Truth concealed and covered up causes people to be alienated from self. Not-knowing allows something to come between the self and self-conscience (or God) which

70

allows someone else to control the life of the self. The disciplines of the ancient Kemetic "mystery" religion provided the truth of human nature that would "bind the self to the self." Had Jesus been allowed to live and get this message out completely (for the ancient original ways was his birthing), or had Islam not been met with resistance and military opposition (Crusades) when Prophet Muhammad and his successors began to awaken people to their own inner power and the need to submit to the natural laws in the way of Allah ("Who is closer than the jugular vein" says the Holy Qur'an), American people (and the West in general) would not be in such a helpless condition as it is today. It is a condition of gullibility and naivete whereby the very nature of the people is exploited because they do not know the composition of self and human nature. Thus the very integrated and cohesive system of initiation in the ancient Kemetic way (in which Jesus and Muhammad both were rooted) would yield a human being who had full possession of knowledge of self and that of the universe as well. The holy teachers knew this; so did their enemies. The universe of self and the world around are based on and rooted in the same principles of natural order and law.

As people become more reflective and are able to see the harm in habits and addictions they possess, they are closer to self control and resisting those who would capitalize off their ignorance. It is then that the corporate establishment must become more sophisticated in its strategies of control. They simply do the counter-capitalizing tactic mentioned before and generate needs for "treatment" and "cure." Even when people recognize danger and destruction, they often doubt their own abilities to handle the "treatment." Thus, the industrial capitalists move in and offer products: smoking clinics, weight reduction classes, exercise formats, sleeping apparatus (waterbeds, reclining chairs in which one can relax, eat, sleep, cure disease, etc.),--no one ever, among those interested in exploiting a need, instructs the people to rely on themselves.

And so it is that the Eurocentric frame of mind, this worldview, essentially had rendered man not only sinful and in need of salvation, but without the means whereby he or she can successfully live life unless they tap in on available expertise and accompanying products of cure and salvation.

In his time of rule, 6,000 years, the white man has fulfilled the prophetic warnings of what to expect of him. He was "made" to rule the earth by means of deception and force. Elijah Muhammad quotes Genesis 1: 26-28, as referring to the making of the white man:

And God said: "Let us make man in our image, after our likeness: Let them have dominion over the fish of the sea; over the fowl of the air; and over the cattle, and over all the earth; and over every creeping thing that creepeth upon the earth:" and God said unto them: "Be fruitful and multiply; and replenish the earth, and subdue it."

This was how the white man was to rule, not the Native American (Indian) who submitted to the laws of the universe, nor the original Asiatic-African peoples who built civilizations long before Yakub on the principles of universal laws.

If we follow the Yakub narrative as presented by the Honorable Elijah Muhammad, we find that the white man lost all sense of shame and fundamental principles of human behavior during his time of exile in Europe (that is, west Asia later known as Europe or Europe --meaning they were roped off from the holy black lands of east Asia- Africa). Says Elijah Muhammad :

Yakub's race of devils were exiled in the hills and caves of West Asia (now called Europe). They were without anything to start civilization and became savages. They remained in such condition for 2,000 years—no guide or literature.[25]

The Europeans remained this way until Moses was sent to them about 2,000 years later, in an effort to "raise" them in knowledge and the principles of civilization.

In time, the white man emerged to build the white civilization with the little knowledge and skill he gained from this period of "raising" or "civilizing". The world he would build would be based on sheer deception and mastery. It was the only way he knew, (the biblical story of Jacob stealing his brother's birthright is related here). What white America is really all about is a drama with two narratives going on at the same time. The Native Americans foresaw this when they said the white man had a forked tongue. It is more sophisticated than blatant hypocrisy, though that's apparent, too. It involves consistent pronouncement and concealment; confession and cover-up;

avowal and disavowal.

In short, the cover-ups continue by virtue of the fact that the white man embraces what he in fact denies; or denies what he in fact embraces. He claimed Jesus in order to rid the world of him; he declares a war on drugs, but is involved in the use and importation of them. The white man always has to disseminate two stories anytime he wishes to communicate, because he started out with a lie (that is, stealing the birthright of original people and claiming superiority, thus white supremacy). And as anyone familiar with a liar knows, a second lie is always needed to cover up the first one.

It is this capacity to deceive, to "put on" while "pulling off," to" appear" on one level, while disappearing on another; the craft of prevarification, that has entitled the white man to the station and name of "devil." Webster says the one who prevaricates "walks crookedly." He sways and wanders from the truth. Proverbs says "he winks."

THE ARCHDECEIVER AND THE WINK

Proverbs says, in the Gideon Bible, "a naughty person-- he winketh his eyes." The New Jerusalem version puts it this way:

> *A scoundrel, a vicious man,*
> *he goes with a leer on his lips,*
> *winking his eye, shuffling his foot,*
> *beckoning with his finger.*
> *Deceit in his heart, always scheming evil,*
> *he sows dissension. Disaster will overtake him sharply for*
> *this, suddenly, irretrievably, his fall will come.*
>
> *Proverbs 6: 13*

Elijah Muhammad described the archdeceiver as follows:

> *That old serpent, called the devil and Satan, which deceiveth the whole world (Rev. 12-9) is a person or persons whose characteristics are like that of a serpent (snake). Serpents or snakes of the grafted type cannot be trusted; they will strike you when you are not expecting a strike.*[26]

73

The serpent of the grafted type is the white man, and it was the teaching of Elijah Muhammad that because of this genetic grafting (or alteration) it was not in the white man's nature to be truthful and righteous. While some may develop a character which in fact demonstrates submission to conscience, to the laws of nature and acts of generosity and kindness, this according to Elijah Muhammad, would be because of the person's reflection and reconsideration, and not because it was his inherent nature. Doing right then would be a decision; not a compelling drive and unreflective directive that springs from the heart and soul itself as it did with the original man.

The conduct of the white man throughout history has borne out the analysis put forth by Elijah Muhammad. Whether one accepts this analysis as valid or not, the evidence demonstrates that in general, the white man more often than not, has a trick up his sleeve. He never comes at you straight; he always is cloaked in deception, disguise, and in cunning.

The white man is one who winks. It is the sign of deception. Consider the child's story: "Winkin', Blinkin', and Nod." It tells the truth in a way the author may never had intended. The deceiver winks; the believer (of the deceiver) blinks (accepts and trusts), and then the believer nods (falls into sleep or illusion), or the deceiver nods (to give the go ahead in some conspiracy or collaboration).

It all happens quickly, because the deceiver has plotted both stories going down. As "quick as a wink" he has secured the trust of one who had believed the "public" (upfront) story. We do not know if the Blue Coats, the 7th Calvary, winked at one another when they assured Si Inskokeca (Big Foot) and his weary, cold, and beleaguered Hunkpapas and Minneconjou men, women and children, that when they laid down their weapons at Wounded Knee in 1890, they would be given provisions and safe passage on to the Pine Ridge Reservation. But we do know ''as quick as the wink of an eye," the Blue Coats, that is the U.S. Military 7th Calvary, had massacred three hundred men, women and children once they (the Indians) kept their part of the " agreement. "

We do not know if men like the slave trafficker, John Hawkins, winked at one another when they stood on the shores of Africa and bargained, tricked and kidnapped the native black people to be brought to the Americas as slaves, but we do know that " as

74

quick as a wink," they had managed to secure millions of men and women in slave forts and factories, having deceived them with trinkets, tokens, and rum for the collaborators.

I do not know if the construction company's employer or owner a student recently told me about, winked when he hired Latino " aliens" to do a construction job, and on payday when it came time to fulfill his part of the bargain, as "quick as a wink of the *eye,*" he called the immigration authorities instead.

If we ponder on "the wink" seriously, we can see the whole behavioral construct of the white man. It is the body language of the deceiver. The wink, the smile and the handshake done in succession, are indicators of a double story. The Qur'an says: "And what they have in their hearts is graver stil'".[27]

I began to think on the wink and watched for any mention of it in media. Just in recent newspaper articlesl I ran across the following :

In an article called "Pentagon Probe Airs Layers of Deceit," by Robert F. Howe, it says:

Where a consultant is, by a wink or a nod, telegraphing to corporate executives that they are capable of manipulating the system, tailoring competition exclusively to their client or bribing public officials, that's beyond the pale.[28]

This was said by u.s. Attorney Hudson.

In an article on Oliver North, writer Valerie Richardson reports that "despite three felony convictions, North remains one of the nation's most sought after speakers, even at $25,000 per speech. His ability to raise crowds, not to mention funds, has made him a star attraction on the Republican campaign circuit." Mike Saltser, communications director for the Virginia Republican Party, is reported as saying :

He's a very hot political commodity ... let's just say, if he winks, we'll nod.[29]

In another news brief concerning North, it discussed the Legal Affairs Council, a conservative activist group seeking the pardon of Oliver North, by the then President Ronald Reagan. The Executive Director of LAC, Michael Boos, reportedly asked the President at a private reception "to take care of Ollie North. Please don't leave him hanging." The article went on: "With a wink and a smile, Mr. Reagan replied: 'I will,' according to Mr. Boos.[30]

But the most revealing evidence of the significance of "the wink" that I ran across in the media was an April 20, 1988, article in *The Washington Post* which featured a photo of Attorney General Edwin Meese and President Reagan during a tribute to law enforcement officers who were killed in the fight against drugs. The photo shows Meese winking at Reagan, and the caption reads:

Attorney General Edwin Meese III winks at President Reagan during tribute yesterday to law enforcement officers who were killed in fight against drugs.[31]

Having lost my initial copy of that paper and photo, I went searching for it in the periodical/paper files of a local college library where I taught in another county. After much searching through dates, I found it. The same photo was there, but the caption was different. The article and date were also identical. The caption read: II Attorney General Edwin Meese III and President Reagan at tribute yesterday to law enforcement officers who lost their lives in the fight against narcotics."

I was sure the original version I had seen had the word "winks" in the caption. Some days later, I found the original article in my files and sure enough, the caption was as the first one I quoted. I could only reason that there were different editions printed and sent to various areas of the region. Possibly the editors (and others?) caught the significance of "the wink" being Meese was under scrutiny at the time and they "cleaned up" the caption.

This winking behavior has always signified that another story is about to be written while the familiar one continues on. It is the strategy of the lustful man. This is why he is known by his winking at women. It signified: keep on with the story in progress, but in time another one is going to go down; one that is undercover, out of public scrutiny; it isn't a story for others to know.

This duplicit, hypocritical trait of the white man's relations with people in general could only be maintained because people in general have believed the story given to them. The American Dream ideology is even addictive; it is a story people crave and hold onto because it secures their destiny; it works like all other addictions. Just a little taste of it--a few extra dollars and domestic comfort-- convinces the believer that it is true. The American Dreamers listen to presidential speeches, flock to voting polls, and listen to the evening news with the conviction that it is true--the Dream --because to do otherwise is to cast doubt on the propagators of this ideology; it is to throw shadows across the unblemished characters who seem to epitomize the Dream in flesh. To imply duplicity or fraud, less than noble intentions and motivations, drives spikes into the firm foundation of belief, causing cracks to appear in the world view, the mindset of the believer. Only those who have no reason to believe the fraud, the dispossessed and hungry, the maligned and beleaguered masses of people who are without--only those can initiate the questions.

I am always amazed at young adults who see someone like Benjamin Franklin as a "role model" and character referent. Known as a founding father and as a sober, reasonable man who authored numerous writings that on surface seem to bespeak the virtuous man, Franklin was in fact a very shrewd businessman, an able prevaricator who wrote aphorisms about honesty and thrift while he carried out covert operations of land acquisitions and money making propositions. He paraded publically as an ambassador of goodwill and political acumen, while conducting deals and ventures of personal profiteering in more clandestine backroom kinds of settings. Franklin, who is recognized as one of the architects of the u.s. governmental structure, reportedly took many if not all his ideas for this political formation from the highly developed political system of the indigenous Iroquois Confederacy as articulated in the Great Law of Peace.[32] But he dealt with the indigenous people with characteristic "white supremacy." He applied the tactics of deception and trickery, divide and conquer, with great alacrity and facility. He had a dream of establishing British colonies in the Ohio Valley (in conjunction with other entrepreneurs and economic venturers, such as his own son, William Franklin, Governor of New Jersey). In a letter to his friend, Richard Jackson, dated March 8, 1763, he writes (with a wink?):

Since all the Country is now ceded to us on this Side the Mississippi, is not this a good time to think of new Colonies on that river to secure our Territory and extend our Commerce; and to separate the Indians on this side from those on the other, by intervening Settlements of English, and by that means keep them more easily in order?[33]

This strategy of covert activity, deceptive governance, and illusionary ideology has accompanied the white man's rule throughout history. In America, it has taken on the form of Dream ideology and Democratic rhetoric, while the reality of horror and unjust governance has been testified to and documented by those who never believed, those who believed and woke up, and those who have received the brunt of white American terrorism such as Native Americans, African slaves, and both their descendants.

In the first four chapters of Proverbs, the speaker admonishes his son, his listener, to acquire clear perception. It is the counter strategy for handling the wink and deception. Nowhere has the deceptive strategies of the white man's rule been more graphic and penetrating than in the U.S. Government's secret operations under the Hoover F.B.I., designed to immobilize and ultimately destroy Black, Native American, and young White Leftist organizations which sought political justice and human empowerment. In a series of undercover tactics documented by Ward Churchill and Jim Vander Wall, these agents of deception were able to cause internal distrust and paranoia among the various groups, while wedging their way into militant populations in order to set them up for disintegration and at times assassination. These tactics went under such names as: "eavesdropping, bogus mail, black propaganda operations, disinformation or gay propaganda, harassment arrests, infiltrators and agents provocateurs, pseudo-gangs, bad jacketing, fabrication of evidence, and assassinations."[34]

This craft of deception has been the path of the white man's rule so that he may proceed with activities that defy and negate the just and humane operations of natural law. It 'is this desire to go against nature which has instigated the European's tactics of deceit and concealment.

THE WAR AGAINST NATURE

The craft of prevarication and deception has allowed the white man to ruthlessly, unrelentingly, and systematically go about his business in disregard of basic, universal natural laws. Having either lost or never having possessed that inner mechanism of a check, or a self-accusing spirit, the rudiments of conscience, he has moved across the earth with rapacious greed and disrespect for the inner balance and law of natural phenomena. Everywhere he has gone, he has invaded, aggressed upon, and ultimately destroyed the balanced and peaceful systems of life that were rooted in natural law.

One day as I sat on the banks of a river watching white men cause havoc in the once peaceful waters of the Potomac with their motorized ski-like machines, I thought about how for centuries this typified their behavior. As I observed them zoom over the water's surface, in sport and play, filling the air with a raucous din, and terrifying the aquatic life below as it must have fled in fear to lower depths or shoreline reprieves, I understood how this was just the way white man had entered unknown lands and made contact with indigenous people; as peacebreakers and those who would defy the natural bonds of ecologic harmony.

It was at this same river, only at a different part, that I had witnessed a young white fisherman throw rocks at a trusting friendly duck who had come to get some of the fisherman's bait, having been thrown crumbs and treats by children in the past. A rock caught him in the neck and red began to seep through the pure white feathers. With a terrified "quail," the duck staggered back to the water and managed to make it across a canal to the other shore. It seemed to be looking back at all of us "people" in a pained and hurtful way, for he had been deceived and betrayed, once having grown to trust. I last saw him on a distant shore, his long graceful neck curved down and his bill buried into his chest. I don't know if he lived or not, someone said park police had been called. But the image remained glued in my memory as I watched the white men on their motorized surf machines I remembered the duck.

This white man has no limits. His entire posture towards Mother Earth has been one of assault and rape; violent moments of contact and engagement, whether it be the strip mining of the Black

Hills and Appalachia, or the ripping up of great pinyon (pine) trees in Indian territory for development or the destruction of the rain forests.

Doug Boyd describes in his biography of Rolling Thunder how the great pine nut trees were ripped from their roots, depriving the native peoples of a vital nutritional source, the pinyon nut.[35] The great Paha Sapa (the Black Hills) seemed to cry black tears from the coal slurries as its beautiful terrain would be declared uninhabitable and its aquifers polluted with the presence of multiple uranium mines and coal mines, power generating facilities demanding that the area be "sacrificed" for such "progress."[36]

Not only does the white man ravish the earth in haste as he rips out its coal, uranium, and diamonds, but he leaves in haste, having satisfied his desire, no longer interested in the barren womb once so inviting. All that remain are the signs of his violation: acres and acres of tailings left from the uranium mines; uprooted and massacred trees bound for lumber yards, leaving their birthing soil to erode and wash away with time; the scarred and maimed hides of the manatee, victims of motorized boats that sport and play in the once peaceful waters where they dwelled and spawned their portion of the aquatic life chain around the southern Everglades; the deer carcasses often left in haste after a season of excessive hunting and over-kill; the washed up ale-wives and blue-discolored fish on natul rivers and lake shores, having met the toxic pollution from industrial river-side sites.

Sometimes the carnage is beyond our imagination's grasp; too horrid to visualize and hold in the mind's eye Certainly the victims of lynchings and castration lie he as well as the millions lost in wars such as Vietnam, where mines not only killed but left legless and armless humans as is the case in the aggressions of the U.S. today in Cent America. All one has to do is view the photographs a film clips of Japanese victims of the atomic bomb shown Dr. Helen Caldicott's controversial film, "If You Love This Planet."

Sometimes the slaughter of unknowing animals is equally as graphic. In the video, "Broken Rainbow,"[37] there are scenes showing how agents of the United States Government shot the sheep of Navajo sheepherders their effort to force the Navajo to relocate from the la area in dispute. This is land rich in mineral resources al coveted by both the Government and private industrialists and contractors.

The sheep slaughtered were left mutilated bloodied carcasses near the hogans of ti native people.

In 1988 there were reports of a deer massacre involving an air force base and civilians. It was estimated that the herd numbered about 1500 and had been allowed pasture for 18 years near the base and academy. They hi grown to trust the military members and employees apparently and wandered very close to the facilities. TI deer were ordered to be shot because "they damage parade grounds, shrubs and other facilities" as well causing car accidents.[38]

How do human beings deal with those who have r limits, no *criterion* for behavior except expediency, greed and appetitive gratification? What does one appeal to the white man? It is perhaps this recognition that one is dealing with something in human form but is not and acts not human, which is most overwhelming and terrifying. For, it is the *perception* of the reality you are confronted with that confirms the truth of it. And it is not easy, certainly not pleasant, to confirm and admit that one is dealing with a beast--a devil. Elijah Muhammad did not improperly refer to the white man as the devil; he accurately and truthfully identified him for all to see.

The tragedy of course is that anyone can learn the way, the strategy of the white man; any color, age or gender. Unknowing and easily led people can quickly adapt the behaviors of deception and ultimately of human disregard. There are thousands and thousands of young people now reared on the white man's images of success and well-being. They are mesmerized by the material trinkets of the world he has built. and driven by unchecked and artificial appetites, implanted in their minds and bodies by the white man's advertising tactics and mediated seductions. These youth are capable now of destroying others in order to *get;* in order to *be* what the pictures say one ought to be. The pictures in the mind roll by the conscious sensors of young, grasping psyches that reach for identity, recognition and membership among those they want to be like, be with. They want to be the pictures in their mind, so they learn the ways to be in the picture, how to get into the story, to be somebody everyone will recognize.

Deception is just the beginning, the threshold of some further violation of natural boundary and ecological balance. So far, the western world, built and maintained by the craft and design of white men utilizing slave and exploited labor, has yet to evoke a culture worthy of *human* relation; has yet to establish a climate of human growth and unfolding. It has been, in Elijah Muhammad's words, the rule of the devil.

Certainly there are those who will counter that not *all* Caucasian men act in such a way. And I would reply again; not all Caucasian men have to be white. But we have to recognize the prevailing "type" of character that describes the time of white rule.

I do not remember my father as such a "white man." I'm sure he was in some ways; after all, he grew up in Kentucky during the aftermath of slavery and the era of segregation. He was never known for challenging the system. But I remember him as a man who had a deep love for nature, a kindness towards life. He would bring newborn baby lambs into our kitchen in the cold of winter when their mothers were sick or could not nurse them, and he himself would heat milk and feed them through a doll baby bottle or eye-dropper. He would not allow the quail to be hunted and shot, and he refused to see old Blue, a cow who bore several sets of twin calves to be sold or slaughtered, but let her live out her life naturally on the land she had been for ten years or more. He lived out his life eventually on the margins of the white man's world, forgotten largely by the white men who had known him.

There's my recently departed spiritual brother and long time friend, Robert E. Morrison, who wrote in his first book, *Primitive Existentialism:*

> *Once again, Man is in jail. Once again, human wisdom is called upon to liberate Man form a paramount jailer, form an absolute tyranny, and from the false prophets that are always in attendance upon absolute tyrants.*
> *Once again, a great revolution is afoot in human thinking, a violent revolution to set man free, to set free that creature who appears dedicated to spending its life in jail.*"

Bob Morrison consistently defied the structures and rule of white men, and lived out his life as well on the margins, not unlike my father. But Morrison had an incredible weapon: words. In his trilogy of novels, *Bird of Fire, Mary,* and *Behold, This Dreamer,* the beauty of those words come crashing out, delivering the passion of the destitute, the alcoholic, the youthful free spirit, the prostitute, the poet --all aiming for liberation. How sad that white America never really listened.

But his "students" did those like Bob Johnson who followed the spirit and inspiration of his mentor as he learned to cherish the wisdom and beauty of Native indigenous peoples, the Indian way. Defying the legacy of white supremacy, he has devoted his life to the study and collection of objects embedded in the once gentle ways of the old people.

Peter Matthiessen seems to have long ago left "the white way," perhaps never having been trapped within its mindset. His writings on Native Americans have been widely respected by them as well as those who are not Native people. In writing about the "old way" among Indian nations, Matthiessen makes the point that there is no word for "religion" in native tongues:

Nature is the "Great Mysterious," "the religion before religion," the profound intuitive apprehension of the nature of existence attained by sages of all epochs, everywhere on earth: the whole universe is sacred, man is the whole universe, and the religious ceremony is life itself, the miraculous common acts of every day. Respect for nature is reverence for the Creator, and it is also self-respecting, since man and nature, though not the same thing, are not different.[40]

I wrote Matthiessen and asked him if he would express in writing some account for his NOT being "white' in his mind and conduct towards the universe. In his expected zenlike humble way, he declined but wished me well on the project of this book. Matthiessen turned to Zen Buddhism as a way of life, though he mentioned he would have gone the way of native peoples had there been an opportunity, some path he could have embarked upon.[41]

Not to be forgotten is a Muslim brother out of upstate New York, Harold Zinc, who shared a short moment of Muslim community and landed independence with us in Sedalia, N.C., where the brothers and sisters were trying to establish a Muslim college. Harold's devoted commitment to the effort from feeding the goats to making prayer could not be forgotten.

There's Wendell Berry down in Port Royal, Kentucky, making his stand on a piece of land and with a pen in his hand when not farming. He writes:

> *You can best serve civilization by being against what usually passes for it.* [42]

And,

> *...the white race in America has marketed and destroyed more of the fertility of the earth in less time than any other race that ever lived. In my part of the country, at least, this is largely accounted for by the racial division of the experience of the landscape. The white man, preoccupied with the abstractions of the economic exploitation and ownership of the land, necessarily has lived on the country as a destructive force, an ecological catastrophe, because he assigned the land labor, and in that the possibility of intimate knowledge of the land, to a people he considered racially inferior; in thus debasing labor, he destroyed the possibility of a meaningful contact with the earth.* [43]

Berry has committed himself to the proper relationship with the earth and has devoted years to that effort in teaching, writing, and farming. Though he has not been known for any political challenge to the capitalist system, nor is he called a "revolutionary," his words seem to be both these things and they are in the way of righteousness. There have been some Caucasian male students in my classes through the years who did not fit the "white man" image or behavior --few to be sure. I always wondered about the future for them and the tremendous odds it held against them if they continued to try to be human more than white. Bill Huff comes to mind, with his deep respect and I would say love for Malcolm X, and his sincere interest in Islam. Joseph Nevins is another, whose astute analyses of western politics and aggressions separate him from the typical white male syndrome; as well as his comment that he hoped Blacks would not become white, and would come up with some better way than Whites had established.

Our departed brother, who embraced and fought for the homeless, Mitch Snyder, proved his stand for justice with clear and distinct concrete bodily acts. I recall in an interview he gave to a local college newspaper, his saying that the rules or principles on which this society were founded and operated are absurd and insane --totally against human community.

Lastly, Papa Luke (as we called him) not only is an anomaly, but a wholesome respite in the carnage and pollution of the western world. A former cotton mill worker, military veteran, at an age of approximately 70, devoted his time and energy to the cause of victims of Brown Lung disease (byssinosis) in North Carolina. He had no fear of standing up to the monolithic cotton mill industry, nor of befriending and offering refuge to both my husband and me in times of hardship. He was neither paternalistic nor patronizing towards Black people whom he befriended. In deep reflection, he would ponder these artificial divisions, always returning to his basis for doing anything: human compassion.

Who is to say why these men, and maybe others, don't seem white? Elijah Muhammad said clearly there would be some with good intentions and who would submit to the truth. The above mentioned men, however, did not conceive nor build the white man's world, and we have yet to see if the likes of them can bring about any significant change, though it may be too late. Certainly, any Caucasian man (or woman) who sincerely departs from the "great white way" can only come into clarity and vision through the eyes of non-white human beings; that is, must see as the Native American sees: with balance; and as the African slave descendant sees: with ancient wisdom and human perfection as the goal of earthly life, in obedience and submission to the one source or Creator of the natural universe.

NOTES

(Chapter Two)

1.) *See Message* to *the Blackman in America, op. cit.,* p. 110.
2.) James Baldwin, *The Fire Next Time, op. cit.,* p. 118.
3.) Eldridge Cleaver, *Soul* on *Ice* (N. Y .: Dell Pub. Co., a Delta Book, 1968), pp. 176-190.
4.) Cheikh Anta Diop, *Precolonial Black Africa* (Westport: Lawrence Hill & Co., 1987), p.13. (Tr. by Harold J. Salemson)
5.) *Washington Post,* "Troops Ordered to Calm Virgin Islands" (September 21, 1989).
6.) *Message* to *the Blackman in America, op. cit.,* p. 116.
7.) Ibid
8.) *See Washington Post* (August 15, 1989)
9.) *Ibid.*
10.) J.R.H. Moore, *An Industrial History of the American People* (N.Y.: The MacmillanCo.,1918),pp.23-24.
Ibid., p. 24. Apparently the word *rum* originated from a Devonshire word, *rumbullion,* meaning "a great tumult." (See Academic American Encyclopedia). I have witnessed myself the "fire' of rum while living in Kingston, Jamaica, and sit ting in hospital waiting rooms where I saw men undergo "rum fits, a seizure like condition often causing hospitalization. Deaths at a premature age for men were not uncommon.
12.) Moore, *An Industrial History, op. cit.,* p. 126.
13.) W.E.B. DuBois, *Suppression of the African Slave Trade, op. cit.,* p.29.
14.) Clifford Alderman, *Rum, Slaves, and Molasses: the Story of New England's Triangular Trade* p. 49.
15.) *See* Ward Churchill and Jim Vander Wall, *Agents of Repression: The FBI's Secret Wars Against the Black Panther Party and the American Indian Movement* (Boston: South End Press, 1988).
16.) DuBois, *Suppression of the African Slave Trade, op. cit.,* pp. 35- 36; 41; 49.

17.)   Quoted in James R. Granger, Jr., *Adam, the Altaic ring, and the Children of the Sun* (Washington, D.C.: Uraeus Pub., Inc., 1987), p. 195. *See* Echewa's original article in *Newsweek* (July 5, 1982), p. 13.

18.)   Judith Mackay, "The Tobacco Epidemic Spreads," in *World Health* (The Magazine of the World Health Organization, October, 1988), pp. 9-12.

19.)   *Ibid.*, p. 12.

20.   *The Burning Spear* (Publication of the African People's Socialist Party, January, 1989), pp. 4-5. Since the above address was given, it has been reported that John Hull has fled the country of costa Rica (where he is a naturalized citizen), and is somewhere in Miami. On January 12, 1989, Hull was arrested by the Judicial Investigation Organization on charges of espionage, violating Costa Rican neutrality, arms smuggling, and narcotics trafficking. *See Mesoamerica* (a publication of the Institute for Central American Studies, August, 1989; February, 1989). Also see the following issues for further references on Hull: *Mesoamerica* (Vol. 3, Nos. 5 and 10; Vol 5, Nos. 2 and 6; Vol. 6, Nos. 5 and 6; and Vol. 7, No. 6).

21.)   *The Burning Spear, op. cit.* , (January, 1989)

22.)   Lisa Leff, "Ultra-Car Stereos Blast Off, *"Washington PoS!* (April 15, 1989) Sections A-1; A-14.

23.)   *Ibid.*

24.)   Susan Dillingham, "Perking Up Sales by Cooling the Coffee," *Washington Times* (May 29,1989).

25.)   Elijah Muhammad, *Message* to *the Blackman* in *America, op. cit..p.119.* .

26.)   *Ibid.*, pp. 122-123.

27.)   *The Holy Qur'an* (trans. by Abdullah Yusuf Ali) Surah 3: 118: "What their hearts conceal is far worse."

28.)   Richard Howe, "Pentagon Probe Airs Layers of Deceit," in *Washington Post.*

29.)   Valerie Richardson, "North's World Full of $25,000 Oysters," in the *Washington Times.*

30.)   "Inside the Beltway" section, in the *Washington Times* (November 11,1988).

31.) *Washington Post* (April 20, 1988). There were apparently dif ferent editions which featured the same story and photographs but different captions. Author is investigating the discrepan cies at the present time.

32.) See Donald S. Lutz, *The Origins* of *American Constitutionalism* (Baton Rouge: Louisiana State University Press, 1988) pp. 126- 129. A thorough consideration of the subject is Bruce E. Johansen's *Forgotten Founders: Benjamin Franklin, the Iroquois, and the Rationale for the American Revolution* (Ipswich, Mass., 1982). Also back issues of the Mohawk Nation's publication *Akwesasne* Notes. And chap. 8 of Jack Weatherford's *Indian Givers: How The Indians* of *the Americas Transformed the World (N. V. : Fawcett Columbine,* 1988).

33.) Letters to Jackson, Papers X, 209, as quoted in Esmond Wright, *Franklin* of *Philadelphia* (Cambridge: the Balknap Press of Harvard University Press, 1986), p. 132.

34.) *Agents* of *Repression, op. cit.,* Chapter 2.

35.) See Doug Boyd, *Rolling Thunder(N.Y.:* Random House, 1974), p. 73 ff .

36.) See *Agents* of *Repression, op. cit.,* Chapter 4.

37.) "Broken Rainbow,.. an Earthworks production of film by Maria Florio and Victorio Mudd. Direct Cinema Limited, P.O. Box 69799, Los Angeles, 90069.

38.) *Washington Post* (October 16, 1988)

39.) Robert E. Morrison, *Primitive Existentialism* (N.Y. : Philosophical Library, Inc., 1967), p. 1. The trilogy of novels mentioned in the text were published as the first three vol umes of a quintet called *The City* of *Light* (N. Y.: Vantage Press, 1978). The remaining two volumes were in various stages of completion at the time of his death.

40.) Peter Matthiessen, *Indian Country* (N. Y .: Viking Press, 1984), p. 9 ff.

41.) See his *Nine-headed Dragon River: ZEN Journals,* 1969- 1982 (shambala Pubrs, 1987), p. 180.

42.) Wendell Berry, *A Continuous Harmony: Essays Cultural and Agricultural* (N.Y.: A Harvest/H.B.J. Book, Harcourt Brace Jovanovich, 1971), p. 42. Also, *Recollected Essays,* 1865-

1980 (San Francisco: North Point Press, 1981), p. 281.

43.)   Wendell Berry, *The Hidden Wound* (Boston: Houghton Mifflin Company, 1970), p. 141.

CHAPTER THREE

THE WHITE WOMAN

There is one essential historical fact to keep in mind when considering the white woman: she did not found nor build so-called western (white) "civilization," nor has she ruled it. But in the words of Betty Cofer, once a slave, "she carried the keys to the storerooms and pantries." Betty Cofer was talking about Miss Julia, her plantation mistress, but in another sense she was talking about the white woman in America.[1]

While white women have not constructed the white world, they have been "kept" by it, being allowed domicile and access to its material acquisitions and assets. Being the bearer of keys and the protector of the white man's profits and accumulated wealth, she has, in collaboration and complicity, perpetuated the kingdom of white supremacy and the empire of material grand theft.

She was, in essence, an accomplice in the blatant robbery of bonded slave labor, and the many duplicit master plans designed to trick native Americans out of land and sovereignty. While she did not mastermind the invasions and usurpations, she did enjoy the "spoils of war ," so to speak, and seldom refused the bounty which her male protector (keeper) extended to her .

While African women and Native indigenous women were either being enslaved or murdered, white women were in demand to assist the male settlers in "opening" up the frontiers of America. In some cases prostitutes from the old world were imported for predominantly male populated areas on the new frontiers. In order to attract women to new frontiers, the western territories granted wives the right to hold their land separately from their husbands. And in the 1850's, single women in Oregon were given 320 acres if they would migrate there.[2]

It is noteworthy that the former slave and abolitionist, Sojourner Truth, would a few years later appea: profusely to the President and the Congress for lands in the West for the freed slaves, rather than providing them with handouts in major cities to which many of them would flock in search of sustenance. She collected thousands of signatures on petitions for this effort as she tirelessly toured the country, speaking at churches and community halls in her campaign to secure land. Her efforts were to no avail and she died with the petitions reportedly stored in a drawer, never having been seriously considered by Congress. While white women were recruited through gifts or grants of lands, Blacks who had labored in slavery for two centuries preceding, could not get land which was due them in compensation for free labor. Rather, they were rendered "free" but in fact would be continuously colonized and entrapped in rural and urban poverty for centuries to come.[3]

The white women of the nineteenth century who became known for various social welfare reforms and programs, as well as voting rights demonstrations, only helped to perpetuate and maintain the unjust and unequal system erected by their white male counterparts. These women were active in the arena which tolerated their social causes as long as they did not radically alter or dismantle the existing social structure and its institutional network. Neil Irvin Painter says in her commentary on the era of women suffrage movements:

Although women's rhetoric stressed gender, the aim was to heal the injuries of class, and to a very great degree, women's institutions laid down the agenda for the public health and social welfare reforms that in the twentieth century sohened the impact of industrialization on working people.[4]

A city like New York displayed both the finery of these middle and upper class women, and the amazing poverty of the poor immigrant women and black domestics. Who all too soon learned of the harsh reality which offered them little or no employment except the most menial of tasks. The efforts of the middle and upper class women to establish charities to address the needs of the masses of impoverished women did nothing to disrupt or alter the malicious capitalist system which could not stand without the poor population which these women were attempting to assist.

While one would hope that this material disparity due to a

capitalist class structure would motivate the impoverished women to organized rebellion, it seems only to have fired the flames of want and covetousness. Christine Stansell comments on New York in the 1800's:

> *Merchant capitalism shaped the social geography of the city..Lining Broadway, the street of fashion, were the fine town houses of wealthy shippers Dressed to the hilt in the latest British style, trailed about by servants, the New York rich showed a flair for fashion that led travelers to compare the Broadway throng to that of London's Bond Street.*

Stansell goes on to say:

> *Like other single working women, servants were notorious for spending their money on fancy clothes By the 1840's, domestics provided enough business to support a large group of shop dressmakers in the city. The dresses cost two to three dollars—just about a month's wages—and according to the Tribune's sources, some servants ordered as many as eight a year.[5]*

Much of this conspicuous consumption and fashion mindedness in the working women came from their employers who encouraged them to dress well by giving them their cast-off and hand-me-down clothes. And, says Stansell, " a well-dressed servant was an emblem of the employer's own status."

In time, mistresses (employers) resented this unintended effect of their castaway clothes and pressed their servants (domestics) to dress plainly and according to their means. But even to this day, fashion and the display of "good clothes" dominate the consumption habits of all classes of women, having a neutralizing and mitigating effect on any possibility of turning the status of "have-not" into a revolutionary posture.

Of course the mercantile male entrepreneurs were the ones who benefited the most from such material appetites of their female population. Women of all classes were trapped in the web of exploitation, whether by being kept or worked. Says Stansell: " Laboring women were confined within a patriarchal economy predicated on direct dependence on men." This dependency was not so much desirable and pleasurable as it was inevitable. "If women were parasitical dependents, then they lived in men's households on sufferance."[6]

Thus white women did not seek to dismantle the class system nor the industrial empire white men had established. Instead, those who did display some degree of social conscience, sought human reform in a system of work already destined for dehumanization, given its goal of profiteering and its mean of exploited human labor.

DEPENDENCY AND PLANTATION POWER

When we consider the institution of slavery, the white woman in the South assisted in its administration, was ohen in charge of its daily routines in the absence of the master, and came to depend on it freely for everyday survival and domestic comfort. While some slave mistresses might have sought to ease the burden of their slaves, they did not engage in any significant effort to dismantle or destroy the institution. Most assumed the title and posture of "mistress" with callous determination, sometimes rivaling the master's inhumane devises against the slaves who were in his command.

A slave woman recalling her childhood to an interviewer during the nineteenth and twentieth century collections of slave narratives, said :

I recollects once when I was trying to clean the house like Old Miss tell me I finds a biscuit, and I's so hongry I et it, 'cause we never see such a thing as a biscuit only sometimes on Sunday morning. We just have corn bread and syrup and sometimes fat bacon, but when I et that biscuit and she comes in and say, "Where that biscuit?" I say, "Miss, I et it 'cause I'm so hungry. Then she grab that broom and start to beating me over the head with it and calling me low-down nigger, and I guess I just clean lost my head 'cause I knowed better than to fight her if I knowed anything't all, but I start to fight her, and the driver, he comes in and he grabs me and starts beating me with that cat-o'-nine tails, and he beats me till I fall to the floor nearly dead. He cut my back all to pieces, then they rubs salts in the cuts for more punishment. Lord, Lord, honey! Them was awful days.[7]

Thus the slave mistress not only collaborated with the master in the "peculiar institution" of slavery, but every nale given to her protection and security would join her in 'xecuting the authority she assumed by being an appendage of the master. This slave woman recalls:

Marsa was a well-meanin' man, but ole Missus was a common jog. She put a piece of candy on her washstan' one day. I was bout eight or nine years old, an' it was my task to empty the slop ev'y mornin'. I seed dat candy layin' dere, an' I was hungry. Ain't had a father workin' in de fiel' like some of de chillum to bring me eats--had jes' little pieces of scrapback each mornin' throwed at me from de kitchen. I seed dat peppermint stick layin' dere, an' I ain't dared to go near it cause I knew ole Missus jus' waitin' for me to take it. Den one nornin' I was so hungry dat I cain't resist. I went straight in lere an' grab dat stick of candy an' stuffed it in my mouf...

The slave girl ate the candy and later was questioned by he mistress. This is what the mistress proceeded to do as punishment:

Well, she got her rawhide down from de nail by de fire place, an' she grabbed me by the arm an's she try to turn me 'cross her knees whilst she set in de rocker so' she could hold me. I twisted an' turned till finally she called her daughter. De gal took dat strap like her mother tole her and commence to lay it in real hard whilst Missus holt me. I twisted 'way so dere warn't no chance o' her gittin' in no solid lick. Den old Missus lif' me up by de legs, an' she stuck my haid under de bottom of her rocker, an' she must of whupped me near a hour wid dat rocker leg a-pressin' down on my haid. Nex' thing I knew de ole Doctor was dere, and' he was a-pushin' an' digging' at my 'ace, but he couldn't do nothing' at all wid it. Seem like dat rocker pressin' on my young bones had crushed 'em all into soft pulp. I couldn' open my mouf an' dey warn't no bone in de lef' side. I ain't never growed no mo' teef on dat side. Aint never been able to chaw nothin' good since. Been eatin' liquid stew, an' soup ever since dat day, an' dat was eighty-six years ago.[8]

One wonders about the Missus' daughter who learned early on how to execute the *domestic terrorism* that was part of the common order of the plantation day. She would then grow into a "skilled" mistress, and so on through the generations. And even though chattel slavery ended, and the white woman's cruelty was abated in some degree, I sometimes wonder about the common heritage of the succeeding years; wonder about someone like a young white woman student I had in class while teaching at a university in North Carolina. While trying to understand and cope with racial tensions in her own time, she commented in her writing for class: " I just grew up with them in the kitchen."

One also wonders about the psychological construct of women who could witness extreme brutality on the part of their husbands to his slaves, and yet sleep with him, bear his children, and somehow emerge unscarred and mentally balanced as human beings. Think of Mrs. Lynch and Mrs. Hill in the following excerpts from Peter Wood's work on Blacks in colonial South Carolina, when he quotes from Charles Westey's personal journal of that period :

Colonel Lynch cuts off the legs of a poor negro, and he kills several of them every year by his barbarities. Mr. Hill, a dancing-master in Charleston, whipped a female slave so long that she fell down at his feet, in appearance dead; but when, by the help of a physician, she was so far recovered as to show some signs of life, he repeated the whipping with equal rigour, and concluded the punishment by dropping scalding wax upon her flesh: her only crime was overfilling a tea-cup!

The human sensibilities of the wives of these men must have been sorely scarred or dulled to the point that they either actually believed the slaves were not human (though animals deserved no such terrorism either) and justified both their (master and mistress) atrocities; or they realized the slaves' humanity and their spouses' lack of it. Either way, they surely had to be psychologically unbalanced and pathologically dependent on such an institution for their own subsistence and survival.

The slave mistress's own brutality was often heightened by the attraction a slave woman may hold for her husband, the master. His obvious and known lust for the slave women, and his visitations to the female slave quarters could only harden the mistress' heart towards those whom she saw not as rape victims but as secret concubines.

Harriet Brent Jacobs was a slave in North Carolina and recalls how her cruel master, Dr. Flint, exploited the women slaves. And of his wife she said :

Mrs. Flint might have used (her) knowledge to counsel and to screen the young and innocent among her slaves; but for them she had no sympathy. She watched her husband with unceasing vigilance.[10]

The white slaveholding women, then, were locked into an economic and social system that furthered their dependency on institutions devised and administered by white males. The pathology of it was that they lived in degrees of false consciousness which augmented their role as a form of power, when in fact that had no real power at all apart from the master's. This rendered them even more dependent, not just on the men, but on the slave women to whom they would delegate duties.

In her exhaustive research on plantation households, Elizabeth Fox-Genovese makes reference to the same symbols of dependency and appendageness to the white male as Betty Cofer did in her slave narrative. Says Fox- Genovese:

The mistress of the household...assumed the mantle of ruling lady, whether she bore it gracefully or awkwardly. All other women of the household were subordinate to her. As a symbol-of her station, she carried the keys to the innumerable storerooms and domestic outbuildings. " (Emphasis mine)

In a sense, she was merely a trustee of the master and his economic system of slavery. She carried his keys and guarded his storerooms; and in doing so, she lived in the illusion of power and authority. The slave women, however, understood her impotence and knew her for what she was more extensively than she did herself:

Even when slave women worked under a driver or in an all-female group under female supervision, the shadow of the master or the overseer hovered over them.[12]

Few of these slave women were duped, says Fox- Genovese. They understood the face of power quite well : it was white and male.

The white woman's dependency and false consciousness were furthered bolstered by the ever-present population of exploitable labor. As mistress, she could and did delegate duties to slave women "under" her. While she herself could perform some of these tasks, such as sewing, she rarely ever completed all of any task, but oddly enough seemed to see herself as actually doing the work. According to Fox-Genovese:

As in so many other instances, she (the slave mistress) saw herself as doing what was in fact done for her, albeit under her direction. Her attitude paralleled that of the typical planter who would note that he had "ploughed my field."

The slaveholding white woman increased her dependency on others outside her as she delegated more and more duties to female slaves: cooking, nursing, child care.

Nurses, like other female house slaves,...performed most of the labor that the mistress fancied she had done herself.

From the slave's perspective, or any outsider from the "peculiar institution,"slavery as a social system afforded mistresses the possibility of implementing their own responsibilities through the labor of other human beings, who recognized the mistresses themselves as handmaidens of the system as a whole." In short, the white slaveholding woman symbolized as a key-bearer , ultimately gained access to the white man's wealth via such economic strategies. Despite her dependency and entrapment in a male-dominated system, she did consciously live, says Fox-Genovese, as "a privileged member of a ruling class."[13]

White women therefore "rarely challenged the legitimacy of paternal domination directly, even if they covertly resisted its abuses," and, says Fox-Genovese, "their resentment of the abuses rarely passed i nto rejection of the system that established their sense of personal identity within a solid community."[14]

Even the much heralded and more northern leaders of the suffragist movement were appealing for participation in an exploitive, capitalistic socio-economic system rather than organizing to dismantle it. Despite the fact that their movement and "the woman question" arose in direct relationship to the abolition movement against slavery (just as the modern women's liberation movement arose in response to and borrowing from the Black Liberation movement), there were very real and identifiable racist aspects of the suffragist mindset. It was clearly displayed in the National Woman Suffrage Association

(NWSA), led by Elizabeth Cady Stanton and Susan B. Anthony, when they opposed Black male suffrage until white women could first gain the vote. Another faction, the American Woman Suffrage Association (AWSA) saw Black male suffrage as a stepping stone to woman suffrage. Neither held the human rights of Black men or women as a priority in itself.[15]

White women were known to resist the Black man getting the vote before them. They are reported to have argued against it, speaking of "Sambo" and "the ignorant black man whose rights came before those of 'women of wealth, education, and refinement.'" Minutes of the meeting to debate this issue at a gathering of the Equal Rights Association in 1869, included the testimony of a woman lawyer, Phoebe Couzins, who, among other things, stated that Black women were more intelligent than the men, subjected to greater brutalities. And Paulina Davis said Black women were more intelligent than the men because they had learned something from their mistresses. She also related to incidents of Black men whipping and abusing their wives. Elizabeth Cady Stanton drew applause when she said she did not believe in allowing ignorant negroes and foreigners to make laws for her to obey.[16]

The suffrage and temperance movements were mostly led by middle and upper class white women. Thus their attitude towards work and laboring people were class- bound, therefore ultimately racist. Their major goals revolved around their own position within the existing socio-economic system, rather than around issue of human liberation arising from slavery and the genocidal tactics inflicted on Native American populations. These were women who existed in circles of powers, and as always, held keys and trustee-like positions close to the source of power (white men). Harriet Stanton Blatch, Elizabeth Cady Stanton's daughter, in the 1894 suffrage campaign spoke at "parlor meetings" to wealthy suffragists like Mrs. Russell Sage and Mrs. John D. Rockefeller.[17]

It should be remembered that the massacre at Wounded Knee had occured only four years prior to this suffragist campaign. The white women suffragists demonstrated more interest in acquiring power in the very government that had perpetrated both slavery and Native American genocide, than in abolishing that entire system. Even Mother Jones, the intrepid, fiery activist for miners and all poor working men, women, and children, whose hero was reportedly John Brown, failed to carry her protests as far as Brown, nor ever really agitated for it, despite her strong criticism of capitalism and the power of wealthy industrialists.

In hindsight, it is worth noting how few white women seemed to support Brown's activism and revolutionary stand at Harper's Ferry. A good many possibly related to him the way Emily Hawley Gillespie did. She recorded in her diary:

> *Dec. 2, 7859: Today Brown is to be hung in Virginia for meddling with that which is none of his business about Kansas matters. Snow.* [18]

WHITE AMERICA: THE SAFE HOUSE

By the turn of the century and the early 1900's, white women appeared to be just as entrenched in the white supremacist system and the American Dream as the men.

The years following the Civil War, Slave Emancipation, and Reconstruction had brought even deeper and far-reaching racial divisions and white hysteria over the black population's migrations and movement into the American industrial economy as urban workers, or freedmen in the South who sought land and property of their own.

The lynching decades were years of white hysteria and malicious societal oppression. White women wanted the system to work just as their men did; and in time, would be convinced of the Black man's "danger" to them (the rape syndrome) and his perceived efforts to supplant the white man's power. White women, like their male counterparts, witnessed the atrocities of genocide. W.E.B. DuBois reports there were 1700 Blacks lynched in America from 1885 through 1894. 1892 was the zenith of lynching years: 235 persons publicly murdered. DuBois said during the 16 years of his teaching career, nearly 2,000 persons were publicly killed by mobs (and not a single one of these murderers were punished.) [19]

And as the U.S. entered World War I, white women cheered on their soldiers, while growing as a nation in race hatred towards Blacks, who were making inroads into the military as well as urban jobs. Lynchings increased in 1915 and 1916 and by 1917, with heavy migrations of Blacks out of the South into northern cities, the white violence increased, resulting in riots such as the one in East St. Louis, when 125 Blacks were killed by white laborers. Blacks retaliated to this kind of overt racism across the nation. The 24th black infantry stationed in Houston were provoked to the point that they seized arms and killed 17 whites. As a result 13 Blacks were hanged and 41 imprisoned for life.[20]

In the meantime, white women were near gaining power through the vote. They had cast their lot, so to speak, with their male counterparts in supporting and perpetuating an economic and social system based on labor exploitation, racism and sexism. In 1919 there were race riots (rebellions from a Black perspective) in 26 American cities, with scores of Blacks being killed. DuBois reports: "for one day, the city of Washington in July, 1919, was actually in the hands of a black mob fighting against the aggression of whites with hand grenades."[21]

Here is Manning Marables's summary of such events, drawing upon eyewitness descriptions:

The lynchings committed against Blacks in the early twentieth century were designed specifically to evoke this special kind of terror. Walter White described these murders as being "executed with a bestiality unknown even in the most remote and uncivilized parts of the world." Between 191B and 1927, 91.6 percent of all persons lynched in the u.s. were Black. Eleven were Black women, three of whom were pregnant. Forty-four Blacks were burned alive, and 18 others were burned after they had been executed. Some were simply tied to the backs of automobiles and dragged across city streets until they were unconscious. Many Black men were tied down and brutally castrated with knives or axes. In some cases, the families of the intended victims were seized physically, and delivered to the site to witness the series of atrocities. The purpose of the events was not to kill the Negro quickly or painlessly, but to derive sadistic satisfaction from the suffering of something that was less than human. In the twenties, lynchings became popular cultural events, not unlike circuses and dances. Hundreds or white women and children were invited to take part in the festivities. Fingers, ears, and other body parts of Black victims were eagerly seized for souvenirs. (emphasis mine).[22]

The Black man increasingly became the epitome of danger and violence in the eyes of Whites, and white women were propa-

100

gandized to believe they were the targets of violation. Marable points out that " about 90% of all Americans executed for rape between 1930 and 1959 were black, and all but two of the sentences occurred in the South." Citing information gathered by the Institute for Southern Studies, Marable emphasizes that "no white has ever been executed for the rape of a black" in American history.[23] It is not surprising therefore that in 1989 white racist groups have targeted bombs for the alleged rape of a white woman in Atlanta. According to news reports, the group Americans for a Competent Federal Judicial System, sent a letter to Atlanta T.V. Station WAGA stating "she is only one of thousands of innocent white women who have been raped and murdered by inhuman black barbarians."[24]

White women therefore through the nation's history were cast into a false consciousness of being the "fair prize" of men the world over, especially black men. From this perspective the "eyes on the prize" belonged to lustful black men stalking white women. Blinded to the true historical context of their everyday lives, white women in time would grow both in whiteness and patriotism. America became the safe house; and she did indeed carry the keys to its vast storerooms and pantries, though the keys belonged to her master all along. Despite the human efforts of some good intentioned Caucasian women to bring equity into the total society, the vast majority, from the high echelon to domestics, aspired to a comfortable and secure mode of life in the context of the American structure they knew.

There is probably no better example of this than the women of the Jekyl Island Club. Jekyl Island was the southern haven and winter domicile for the wealthy upper crust who largely resided in the North and had accumulated their wealth there. The island had been owned by a family allegedly implicated in the activities of the slave ship *Wanderer,* said to be the last vessel to bring a major shipment of slaves to the U.S. By 1886, the Jekyl Island Club, conceived perhaps along the lines of the prestigious Union Club, was formed and soon to be spending its time in secluded leisure, sport and play. On this southern coastal sea island, the wives of such capitalist giants as Williams Rockefeller, Nathanial Fairbanks, J.P. Morgan and many others epitomized the early 20th Century image of the American white woman. They accompanied their husbands to the lush life on Jekyl Island, displaying the finest of wardrobes and the lifestyle of leisure. There were in fact eight women stockholders in the club who came to the island in the 1920's.[25]

Jekyl island was, in a sense, a microcosm of the U.S. class system, its members and stockholders coming from the top capitalist circles of the nation's cities. The women wore their husband's names with patriotic zeal and familiar pride, descending upon the island with eager anticipation of "the good life." There was, in the word of authors McCash and McCash, "a tangle of family connections," linking wealth and power through marriage and alliances of descending generations, like the Brewsters, Jenningses, Coes, Auchinclosses, Rockefellers, and Norman Jameses. These women were "the American woman" par excellence in the eyes of the rest of American dreaming population. It is noteworthy that these women displayed no awareness nor interest in the slave history of the island; nor did they seem to realize that it was an island in the long chain of other coastal sea islands off the shores of South Carolina and Georgia, where freed slaves not too many years before stood firm and ready to fight to retain the land which they had worked as slaves for centuries. The women of Jekyl island apparently had no knowledge of or recollection of President Lincoln's Field Order # 15 which was issued to grant the land of the sea islands to freed slaves who had worked these lands for three centuries. General Sherman never executed the Order since Lincoln was killed and President Johnson instead granted the land to the former slave masters.[26]

The white women of Jekyl Island claimed their positions of authority and exclusive class power with loyal support and class consciousness. They depended on a retinue of hired servants, from cooks to housekeepers, gardeners, and gamekeepers. The employees who would serve closest to the members of the club on a day to day basis were white, immigrants and first generations Americans. Blacks were hired, but were quartered at a distance, their comings and goings closely monitored. In 1888, for example, the game committee of the club adopted a rule that "all Negro employees shall follow the open roads and paths when coming or going to work."[27]

The same women who would be among the suffragettes at the parlor meeting and open conventions, and the benefactors of social and humanitarian causes in major northern cities, ironically came south to Jekyl Island only to enforce and depend upon the inequities of a segregated servant force and an extended form of slave labor, only now under the terminology of wage labor and hired help. Once again, the white woman emerged as the one who held the keys to the storerooms and pantries of America, only now she carried keys to banks and industrial corporations, despite the fact that she neither owned nor controlled any substantial amount of wealth. In her consciousness she had come to epitomize American womanhood, as evidenced by Carolyn Stickney who dressed as Lady Liberty at a costume ball on Jekyllsland in 1911.[28]

FROM POCOHANTAS TO UNCLE SAM

Things might have been different for Caucasian women in America (and thus for the nation and hemisphere as a whole} had they paid more attention to the Native (Indian) women of America, with whom they must have had some contact before the years of massive relocation, murder, massacre, cultural and biological genocide of Native people by the white European male invaders. It is hard to imagine or piece together the actual psychological mindset that characterized these early settler women, but surely they had some sensitivity towards the different cultural contexts in which they saw native American women and themselves. And had they seen the African slave women in their native homelands before captivity and bondage, white women have witnessed similar social systems as the Native American which empowered women to positions of significan:t import and community respect. One wonders also how much these white women actually saw and heard from their female slaves which either inspired them or intimidated them with regard to their own gender and its powerlessness in the American capitalist system.

Paula Gunn Allen beautifully demonstrates the early native American root of the quest for freedom and justice in her book *The Sacred Hoop*. She documents the native input not only to the American constitutional government, but also its feminist movement of the 19th and 20th centuries. Whether it be conscious or subconscious, this primacy of the native contact, she argues, is more present than not, despite the white Americans' "loss of memory" which she identifies as "the root of oppression." Says Allen :

The earliest white women on this continent were well acquainted with tribal women. They were neighbors to a number of tribes and often shared food, information, child care, and health care.[29]

These early settler women would have therefore seen tribal societies based on spirit-centered, ritualized, and woman-focussed world-views. Even with the diversity of the various tribes, the underlying foundational axiology on which they based their everyday life was one in which spiritual power and awareness were all-encompassing, and the ordering of social relations and daily routines were governed by women, such as the Clan Mothers or Matrons of the Iroquois Nation.

In fact, the Iroquois Constitution (or White Roots of Peace, also called the Great Law of Peace or the Great Law of the Iroquois) specifically designated the economic and decision-making power of the women. Quoting from various works on the Great Law of Peace, Allen emphasizes Articles 44, 45, and 15, which clearly identify the social recognition and empowerment of the tribal women :

The lineal descent of the people of the Five Fires (the Iroquois Nations) shall run in the female line. Women shall be considered the progenitors of the Nation. They shall own the land and the soil. Men and women shall follow the status of their mothers. (Article 44)[30]

Further quotes from the Articles exemplify the tribal women's political power governing the Chiefs. The Matrons were regarded as the heirs of the Chieftainship Titles and, "if a disobedient chief persists in his disobedience after three warnings (by his female relatives, by his male relatives, and by one of his fellow council members, in that order), the matter shall go to the council of War Chiefs. The Chiefs shall then take away the title of the erring chief *by order of the women in whom the title* is *vested* (Article 19) [31] Eventually the clan mothers or matrons would select another of their sons as a candidate and the Chiefs would elect him.

If the "founding fathers" of the United States did copy much of the Great Law of Peace in forming the new government and its constitution (see Chapter 2), they certainly left out the parts granting such power to the women. Nevertheless, early settler white women must have witnessed the actual gynochracy (woman-centered social system) of Native life. The woman-focused society did not at all mean powerlessness of men nor their being dominated by women, but rather a truly flexible spiritually oriented way of life, in which nurturance, respect for Mother Earth, for the youth (future generations), and mutual cooperation characterized everyday life.

It was a rebellion by Iroquois women in the 1600's that further demonstrated and shaped the Iroquois formation Df a governing constitution or body of articles that insured a matri-lineal and matrifocal social system, according to)tan Steiner. The Clan Mothers grew tired of their men ~ngaging in unregulated warring and so they boycotted ovemaking and childbearing. It worked. In the constitution of Deganwidah the founder of the Iroquois :onfederation, it is said :

He caused the body of our mother, the woman, to be of great worth and honor. He purposed that she shall be endowed and entrusted with the birth and upbringing of men, and that she shall have the care of all that is planted by which life is sustained and supported and the power to breathe is fortified: and moreover that the warriors shall be her assistants. [32]

Steiner also points out that Susan B. Anthony some 2 1/2 centuries later convened a suffragist convention almost on the exact same site (Senaca Falls, N. Y.) as the Iroquois women's rebellion.

For the most part, white feminists failed to penetrate and appreciate the tribal women's truly powerful and equitable way of life as being a model to which they could aspire or attempt to institute. An exception was Eva Emery Dye, an early suffragette from Oregon who chose the Native woman Sacagawea as a feminine image who symbolized the power of women. Sacagawea reportedly traveled with the Lewis and Clark expedition, often acting as translator, and according to Dye, was a moving force on the white settlement of the west. Even Dye seemed to have failed to appreciate the real power of Native women which was rooted in their matrilineality and the focality of them as decision-mak:ers in the community. Dye saw Sacagawea as a friend of white people and an assistant you could say to white male invaders as they explored and settled Native lands. From this point of view, Sacagawea would be seen as a collaborator with the oppression and removal of her own people. But Dye saw her activity as meritorious just as she must have seen the "opening of the west" meritorious. Sacagawea was very young (a teenager) though she had an infant son, and probably had no awareness of collaboration nor the impending dangers to Native peoples on the whole. More troubling is Eva Dye's honoring her for her activities with Whites rather than her indigenous position as a Native woman.[33]

It is not widely known nor made an essential part of American history books and classes that the first symbol of America was a Native American woman. According to Alton Ketchum, the biographer of "Uncle Sam," the Indian youth, Pocohantas, was the first symbol of America. Apparently it was cartographers who drew maps of the New World that selected Pocohantas. Her images frequently adorned maps well into the 1700's.

Later in the 18th Century, pocohantas began to change into the goddess of liberty, as envisioned by the Greek influenced European mindset. Says Ketchum :

> *pocohantas' scanty garb was replaced by flowing raiments of chaste white. And more and more she was called Columbia, a lame some had urged for the nation when the government vas formed.*[34] *(emphasis mine)*

The pure, chaste, delicate and more refined image of the ..hite woman can be seen surfacing in *the* racist collective lindset of the American people with this change of mblems. And Alton Ketchum reveals his own racist ssessment of the gradual transformation in national mblems in the following passage:

> *Our goddess of liberty has been so costumed and identified ~ver since (the 18th century) representing the purer and more dealistic aspects of the American Dream. She is the custodian Ind exemplar of the ultimate values in which Americans le/ieve. (Emphasis mine)*[35]

In time, Pocohantas faded into lost memory as white Americans, both men and women, charged ahead into centuries of more conquest and aggression against Native peoples, African slave descendants, other non-Europeans immigrants, and nature itself. New World capitalism built its empire, and Pocahontas no longer symbolized the whores of America, but was replaced by the European featured, whitened Statue of Liberty and Thomas Crawford's 19-foot figure of Freedom which is atop the Capitol in Washington, D.C.*

But Columbia and the Statue of Liberty were not to hold their place of national identity and governmental authority for long; Yankee Doodle came in as a first male symbol, originally a bumpkin kind of symbol, object of ridicule, raw immigrant stock, uncouth and totally opposite the British mannerisms of refinement. He grew into a more mature, refined "Brother Jonathan," and after the War of 1812, Uncle Sam emerged as the nation's emblem: a patriotic, strong-willed individualist who would come to stand for the U.S. Government itself. Uncle Sam became a kind of omnipotent authority figure that loomed over national activities in an aura of supreme power, whether it be through its familiar finger pointing call to the army, or its presence with the stars and stripes on foreign soil.

At the time this book was going to press, the research of Jack Felder on the original statue of liberty (modelled with a black face) came to ny attention. See TNNN & C Jan/Feb. 1991 issue.

So, there we have it: an almost uncanny symbolic transformation from a Native indigenous female emblem of power, to a white male emblem of domination and militarism. More importantly, this gradual evolution of symbolic emblems is descriptive of what actually occurred in the society and culture of North America: white men and women soon prevailed over the indigenous peoples and their ways of life which centered around principles of matri-focality and human equity.

As I reflect over the past, over women I've known, some I have read, and many more I've taught --few stand out as NOT being characterized by the white woman attributes described in the preceding. I suspect there are quite a few who are unknown, unrecognized in what Elise Boulding calls "the underside of history." White women, it seems, when not consciously wanting to support the social system erected and bestowed upon them by white men, move into a kind of social marginality, dedicating their time to social and humanitarian causes which help alleviate suffering but do not alter nor threaten the economic- social structure which has so dehumanized the conditions of life. My mother and sister would probably be among such women.

Dorothy Day comes to mind, the intrepid founder of the *Catholic Worker* movement (inspired by Peter Maurin's communalistic ideology and counsels) which promoted communal living, cooperative (socialistic) economics, and severe criticisms of the existing social order. But Day, despite her brushes with the law in public protests, lived in mystical world fostered in her adherence to Catholicism (though not in the good graces of the Church), and this seemed to prohibit her from organizing to destroy the roots of oppression, though it motivated her to house and feed the poor long before the Homeless situation had reached such epidemic numbers today. Even so, her many deeds or charity and appeals for justice in the newspaper *(Catholic Worker)* separated her from the Jekyllsland Club types and the bulk of bourgeois white women.

Credit is due to Mother Jones, despite the fact that she seemed to maintain viable relations with the very governmental and industrial male figures she so often indicted publicly. Her stints in jail, and unrelentless protests on the part of miners, and workers in general, somehow separated her from the white women syndrome so prevalent in America. Though she has been criticized strongly by white feminists for not strongly supporting the suffragist movement, Mother Jones it seems saw the movement more clearly than they even today. She complained that women who had achieved the right to vote in several states were not using it for social justice. And she certainly departed from the suffragist appeal for equity in the social system, when she indicted that very system in the following words spoken after her visit at a rope factory in Tuscaloosa, Alabama, around 1901 :

I can see no way out save in a complete overthrow of the capitalistic system, and to me the father who casts a vote for the continuance of that system is as much of a murderer as if he took and pistol and shot his own children [36]

And not to be forgotten in contemporary times is the strong voice of Penny Hess, Chairwoman of the African People's Solidarity Committee. In her attempts to organize North Americans (white people) in support of and in solidarity with the Black Liberation Movement, Hess states:

We have a choice to say,"I break with the U.S. government. I break with white power. I take responsibility for the fact that I am a child of the slave master. and this is the role that I will play to overturn the system.[37]

Those words were spoken at a Conference Against Racism which was held in Berkely, California on July 71 1989. In response to a question about violence, Hess adequately outlined the violence of the American capitalistic social system, and reminded her audience that as long as we function in this system and do nothing to end it, we uphold that violence:

We have to recognize that we uphold the violence, and that our responsibility is to support the struggle for Black Power, to end this system. That is what human life is about, about humanity.

Hess's voice indeed is strikingly a lone voice it seems, amid the far more publicized and popular versions of women's advice and statements about making it in the existing corporate world. These articulations are subtly deceptive in that they speak mostly about implementing genuine feminine attributes into a heretofore macho world of male controlled corporate America. The call to be "women "In su ch co rpo rate cond iti o ns so u nds revolutionary to many unaware women, but it in fact only serves to further the dependency of women in general on white male structures and certainly does nothing to eliminate the inequities and inhumaneness of such structures that were built and continue to be built on exploited labor, white male accumulations of wealth at the expense of non-white labor and lives and subtle appeals to assimilate women into these structures on oppressive male dominated terms. Here is an example. Lois Wyse, President of Wyse Advertising in New York, says while being "all-woman" has worked for her, realistically it won't work everywhere--yet:

Realistically, you are just not going to get to be president of General Motors speaking in an authentic woman's voice, because the men are just not going to let us in. We're going to run service businesses, we're going to run creative businesses, but in my lifetime I will not see a woman be chairman of General Motors unless some nice guy leaves her enough stock to assume control.[38]

What a sad commentary from one who is alleged to be the "new" liberated woman, the career woman. White women in America are hopelessly lost, and this is why Penny Hess's voice stands almost alone; most white women still want to carry the keys to the storerooms and pantries of the white man's empire.*

Is there any way out of this then for Columbia (Lady Liberty) and Uncle Sam? When Elise Boulding says, "for women not to recreate what men have wrought, they will need continually to draw on their underside experience,"[39] I'm afraid she believes that women have seen the value in their forced cooperative economic and neighborhood experiences when confronting poverty, households headed by themselves, and children to be mothered. But my observations have shown me that white women in America do not know themselves nor the men who have created their conditions of dependency; and until they look deeply into the roots of white supremacy, they will continue to want what the white man has. White women need to understand that their underside condition is due to the white man's aggressions against non-white peoples the world over, and that the keys which will unlock the door of freedom, justice and equality, lie not in the storerooms and pantries of America, but in the vast and ancient wealth of African and Native American spirituality and human wisdom that preceded any of the structures in which white people find themselves.

*Dr. Helen Caldicott, Australian born, is one of the most powerful voices today indicting the white male formed and managed system of Western power. She has devoted her medical knowledge to the foundation of Physicians for Social Responsibility, in an effort to deter nuclear porliferation and war, and WAND, an organized effort to mobilize women in the struggle to save Mother Earth.

NOTES

(Chapter Three)

1.) Belinda Hurmence, ed., My *Folks Don't Want* Me *To Talk About Slavery* (Winston-Salem, N.C.: John F. Blair, Pub., 1984), p.70.

2.) June *Sochen,Herstory, Vol.* I, *A Woman's View* of *American History(N.Y.:* Alfred Pub. Co., 1974), p. 114.

3.) See Jacqueline Bernard, *Journey to Freedom: The Story* of *Sojourner Truth.* (N. Y .: W.W. Norton & Co., 1967), p. 261.

4.) Neil Irvin Painter, *Standing at Armageddon: the United States,* 1877-1919(N.Y.: W.W Norton & Co., 1987), p. 252.

5.) Christine Stansell, *City* of *Women: Sex and Class in New York,* 1789-1869 (Urbana: University of Illinois Press, 1987), p. 4; p. 164.

6.) *Ibid.,* p. 18, p. 29.

7.) Dorothy Sterling, *op. cit.,* p. 9.

8.) *Ibid.,* p. 10.

9.) Peter H. Wood, *Black Majority: Negroes in Colonial South Carolina from* 1670 *Through the Stono Rebellion* (N.Y.: W.W. Norton & Co., 1974), p.p. 279.

10.) Sterling, *op. cit.,* p. 20.

11.) Elizabeth Fox-Genovese, *Within the Plantation Household: Black and White Women of the Old South* (Chapel Hill: University of North Carolina Press, 1988)., p.11 0.

12.) *Ibid.,* p. 190.

13.) *Ibid.,* pp. 128; 137; 144-145.

14.) *Ibid.* pp. 101; 193.

15.) Painter, *op. cit.,* p. 242.

16.) Sterling, *op. cit.* pp. 414-415.

17.) Painter, *op. cit.,* p. 246.

18.) Judy Nolte Lensink, *A Secret to* be *Buried: the Diary and Life of Emily Hawley Gillespie,* 1858-1888 (University of Iowa Press, a Bur Oak Original, 1989), p. 26.

19.) DuBois, *Dusk of Dawn, op. cit.,* pp. 29; 48; 55.

20.) *Ibid.,* pp 245; 252.

21.) *Ibid.,* p. 264.

22.) Manning Marable, *How Capitalism Underdeveloped Black America* (Boston: South End Press, 1983), p. 119. 23. *Ibid.,p.121*

24.) *Washington Times* (December 29, 1989) *A* Section.

25.) William Barton McCash and June Hall McCash, *The Jekyl Island Club: Southern Haven for America's Millionaires* (Athens and London: The University of Georgia Press, 1989)

26.) See William S. McFeely, *Yankee Stepfather* (New Haven: Yale University press, 1969), p. 97. Also see Willie Lee Rose, *Rehearsal for Reconstruction: The Port Royal Experiment* (N.Y.: Vintage Books, 1967), and the Freedman's Bureau Records (BRFAL -Record Group 105).

27.) McCash and McCash, *op. cit.,* p. 32.

28.) *Ibid.,* p. 175.

29.) Paula Gunn Allen, *The Sacred Hoop: Recovering the Feminine in American Indian Traditions* (Boston: Beacon Press, 1986), p. 215.

30.) *Ibid.,* p. 212. I would point out the failure of English language to convey the essential meaning, such as in the words "own the land and the soil." Native Americans, no matter the tribe, did not think in terms of private ownership of land as Europeans did. Land was rather in the guardianship of the people and belonged only to the Great Spirit.

31.) *Ibid.,* p. 213

32.) *Ibid.,* p. 213. Allen quotes Stan Steiner extensively, see his *The New Indians* (N.Y.: Dell, 1968), pp. 219-220.

33.) *Ibid.,p.215.*

34.) Alton Ketchum, *Uncle Sam* (1959), p. 10.

35.) *Ibid.,p.11.*

36.) Philip S. Foner, ed. *Mother Jones Speaks: Collected Speeches and Writings* (N. Y.: Monad Press, 1983), p. 455.

37.) *The Burning Spear* (October/November , 1989), pp. 18-19.

38.) Sherry Suib Cohen, "Beyond Macho" in *Working Woman* (February, 1989), p. 80.

39.) For a comprehensive historical and anthropological account of woman, see Elise Boulding's *The Underside of History: A View of Women Through Time* (Boulder, Col. : Westview Press, 1976).

CHAPTER FOUR

ISLAM IN AMERICA

Having looked closely at the white man and woman's presence in history, and having examined the content of white rule and social order {which has really been social disorder}, we can only conclude that the future holds an immense moment of final doom and reparation. The accumulation of unjust aggressions and violations against indigenous non-white peoples of the world, not to mention crimes against the planet earth and natural order, has reached its zenith. Time can only bring destruction, rectification, reparation, and universal reordering of the human family throughout the world.

The Honorable Elijah Muhammad spoke many times of the destruction which would come upon America. In fact, he wrote a book called *The Fall of America*. Drawing upon both Qur'anic and Biblical scriptures, he described how the evils brought to the world during the 6,000 years of white western rule would eventually bring about the downfall of that rule. He also spoke of "the Angry World," which is graphically descriptive of the American human condition today. According to Elijah Muhammad:

The resurrection of the mentally dead black People brings about the anger of those (white man) who put the Black man to mental death. Both people are angry; the Black slave and the slavemaster. The lack of justice to the Black slave is the cause of this anger.[1]

As Black people continue to wake up to the atrocities of the past and the glory of their own African (precolonial} ancestry, they will demand justice to be done; and unless white people desire to submit willingly to the rendering of this justice, we will witness an ultimate, final standoff between black and white, between righteousness and unrighteousness.

Is there then any hope of salvation for the white man and woman? Salvation in the sense of being spared in the final destruction of this social order, and the acceptance by and inclusion with the righteous who will prevail in the hereafter (after *this* world of the white man is destroyed). Elijah Muhammad answered this question on two different levels: one in the concept of grafting; and the other in the way of Islam.

GRAFTING

If we follow the teaching of Elijah Muhammad on the making of the white man (as described in the preceding chapters), we understand that the nature of the white man (the Caucasian) has been "grafted" out of the original. It is, therefore, an aberrant genetic construct and thus lies at the base of the errant and malicious way of white rule and social life. Policies of economic capitalism and the political colonizing of non-white peoples came out of this defective, aberrant form of human construct.

Therefore, on this most fundamental and physiological level, the "salvation" of white people would lie in grafting back to originality (that is, into a righteous nature which is the nature of original black people). Elijah Muhammad explained what he meant by grafting in the following excerpt from *Our Saviour Has Arrived:*

... You cannot change the nature of the white man unless you graft him back into that which he was grafted out of. This is what Jesus means in the Bible In. 3:7 in his conversation with Nicodemus. He told him that in order to enter the kingdom of heaven he must be born again because in In. 8:44 (Bible), Jesus had condemned all of the white race to be devils, and their father was the devil. There was no good nor truth in the father that made the white race. So when a thing is what it is by nature in which it was made or created in, you do not change it unless you go altogether back to the material that it (he) was made out of. So this demands a rebirth. Jesus was right--a rebirth--born again, allover. Some of the clergy and scholars of Christianity take this to be a spiritual rebirth. But it means that the actual flesh and blood that was discussed in this conversation between Jesus and Nicodemus has to be changed. That when the man has been put back into what he was taken from, the spirit of that which he was put back into will come to him as the spirit of evil comes to him now in what he is made in. For he was made out of evil. The white man was not made to obey Allah (God) and to seek after His Righteousness. So, therefore, to make the white man one of the righteous, the white man has to take on a new birth —the flesh and blood has to be

*changed.*²

This fundamental issue of the white man's nature has never been seriously questioned nor explained by white people themselves. Their interest in genetic research has always been from a white supremacist axiology. That is, they would study other ethnic groups from their own perspective to see how close "others' approached white "perfection" and cultural norms. This false consciousness can never be shed until white people confront this fact of genetic mutation (grafting) and the effects it has had on behavior. The very act of confronting the Yakub narrative as presented by Elijah Muhammad would be an initial step in eliminating white supremacy.

This consideration of Yakub takes us back to the question of origins (as delineated in Chapter One) and it is here that Whites must begin in order to uncover, expose and verify the truth of themselves and the original people. This questioning would lead white people out of the clouds of false consciousness (white supremacy) and into the depths of black beginnings, thus the originality and precedence of black civilization long before the emergence of European history and white rule. This very submission to the question of origins of self (kind) in light of Elijah Muhammad's teachings would be an essential step towards a righteous attitude, in that righteousness is truthfulness.

While biochemists have recently asked the question scientifically, utilizing "objective" data (mitochondrial DNA), Caucasian men and women in general need to ask the question inwardly, subjectively (self-consciously) : "What does learning about the originality of Black people and the later making of or emergence of white people mean to *me?*" To confront the Yakub factor destroys the prevailing mindset that either relegates Blacks to savagery and subhuman phenomena, and Whites to godliness; or that lumps all together in some sort of a historical origin point that does nothing to explain the divergence of racial or genetic character.

Even if one refuses to accept or consider the Yakub version of how white people came to be, there still remains the gaping question of how and why the Caucasian genetic mutation occurred, and how it has affected human behavior. The very act of questioning is a rejection of assuming white genetic and cultural primacy. This in itself begins the destruction of white supremacy within the self. It is both an act of destruction (getting rid of the false consciousness) and an act of reconstruction (building a new foundation of truth).

Being Caucasian, and in my own way, a student of the Honorable Elijah Muhammad's teachings, I searched for every word he might have said about the natu re of Caucasians and future doom and/or salvation. For quite a few years I pondered his remarks about this process of grafting. At the time, I understood this concept on a spiritual level only. To me this meant a spiritual reconnection to the original people by way of Islam. But later, upon more careful reading and scrutiny of his words, I realized that he clearly and distinctly meant a genetic, physiological process, in flesh and blood terms.

Thus, an authentic change in the nature of white people would mean a change in genetic terms, just as the making of the white man had been a genetic process of grafting out of the original, it would demand a grafting back into the original. Even as I understood this teaching, I personally did not feel that I was devilish by nature. I concluded this may have had something to do with being raised in a very natural, rural environment by parents who did not display overt kinds of supremacy thinking or behavior, in addition to being raised very close to Black people. But even in childhood, I sensed that the Black people I grew up around were by nature more spiritual and righteous than most of the white people with whom I was associated. And in later years, I truly felt that the African slave descendant who introduced me to Elijah Muhammad's teachings and Islam as such {who later became my husband} was *instinctively* righteous and God- conscious, in his heart and mind.

While environmental, cultural factors serve to augment or diminish how devilish or supremacist one may be, still the genetic construct is a fundamental phenomenon that must be considered and personally researched. This teaching of Elijah Muhammad's on grafting opens up endless questions of cultural and historical import. There are also complex contradictions which need resolution.

For instance, Elijah Muhammad discouraged very strongly the practice of interracial marriage; in fact, this policy was always a part of the Muslim Program which was printed in each issue of the Nation of Islam's paper, *Muhammad Speaks.* The same program is still printed in each issue of the Nation's present-day publication, *The*

Final Call. From this perspective, the intimate intermingling of slave descendants with their former slave master descendants could only continue and perpetuate the interference with and domination of Black people who were in need of being awakened to their true history and self, and a need to "return to their own"--that is, reject a false white- mindedness that would keep Blacks enslaved and prohibited them from attaining personal and collective liberation. Thus, from this view intermarriage would perpetuate the "devil" interference with the original nature of Black people.

But, from a perfectly logical perspective, a Caucasian who might take this grafting solution seriously and from a perspective that saw grafting as a way to return to an original nature, intermarriage would constitute the long- range process of grafting back into the original, and thus would be desirable. In other words, from one view intermarriage would "dilute" and weaken the original genetic construct, but from another view, intermarriage would lead to the absorption and ultimate elimination of whiteness in generations to come and thus end the existential fact of a white race and therefore any possibility of white supremacist thought.

Statistically and existentially Caucasian people constitute only about ten percent of the world's population, and in the United States alone are close to being outnumbered by the growing populations of African and Latino populations especially, along with other non-European peoples. The white supremacist of course fears his or her own genetic elimination, or what Dr. Frances Cress Welsing refers to as "genetic annihilation." The supremacist thus rejects intermarriage. This is why people become confused when they see what appears to be the Ku Klux Klan speaking for the same thing as the Nation of Islam when it comes to this issue. That really is an erroneous conclusion since Klan mentality does not constitute the same attitudinal frame of reference or axiology. The Nation of Islam's program of affirming and returning to black originality and wholeness is not black supremacy, for it has no intent of domination, violation, control, or elimination of other ethnic groups. Rather, it is an axiology of separation, reclamation, and a reunion of people who were interfered with on every level of life by white racists.

Klan mentality, on the other hand, operates out of a fear syndrome--fear of losing white control of the nation's institutions and fear of white people being overrun by dark peoples. Thus the white supremacist in fear will commit genocidal acts against any non-white people who pose a threat (in their minds) to their existence and rule. But the Caucasian who sincerely desires to become extricated from white supremacy and to come into a more human and spiritual nature would logically be drawn to those who exhibit qualities of humaneness; to people who seek justice, who are given to generosity and righteousness; who consult one another in a spirit of harmony and not in plots of deception and discord. Thus, mentally and emotionally, such a Caucasian does not think collectively "white" (we Whites) but seeks to become personally human (beyond color) and separated from a false sense of reality that is based on racial division and illusions of superiority.

When Blacks say "we" (or any non-white peoples who have endured the oppressions and colonization of Whites) it is in a spirit of defense, especially in America--a spirit of being a strong wall of defense against white racism. "We'ness" is this inward power of the people to ward off and combat an oppressive aggressor. "We'ness" is not the same kind of "we" that white supremacists project in a spirit of domination and control. This is beautifully narrated by Mamie Garvin Fields in her Carolina memoir of teaching and community work in a placed called Society Corner on James Island, not too far from Charleston on the mainland. She devotes an entire chapter to this people kind of power that Blacks had to muster up in the face of blatant and overwhelming white racism. She called this chapter "the We Land."[3]

Thus, the Caucasian seeking NOT to be racist has nowhere to turn but to people who are fighting against white supremacy, and in the United States this is Black people, native Americans and some Latino peoples, with a small portion of white people. Because Whites and Blacks have been thrown together from the beginning of the formation of the country on more intimate levels, their proximity makes them more familiar to one another. Caucasians are not as apt to be geographically and culturally close to Native Americans as they are to Blacks, especially in urban areas. However, during the hippie era young Whites did seek out Native peoples to find a way and a vision. In fact, Hopi prophecies foretold of the hippies. Richard Kasti who spoke for the Hopi people at the World Symposium on Humanity in

118

Vancouver, Canada, around 1976-77, reported on the spiritual leaders discussion of these prophecies:

They said we (the Indians) would have visitors, they would be there almost overnight. And the way to recognize them when they came would be that they were peaceful people. They would be going back to the ways of the Earth. They would be making their own food, they would be wearing long flowing hair and beads, they would be having the same kind of problems that the native people have and their name would sound something like Hopi.[4]

It has not been uncommon then for Whites, especially younger white people, to look towards people of color for some kind of way and vision apart from the humdrum bourgeois round of life based on the American Dream ideology.

As a Caucasian involved in an interracial marriage, (so-called), I have reflected on these things for many years and Jnderstand that most mixed unions probably have not been for such clear and rational motives. Many of them through the years have indeed involved the dynamics of racial domination and racial denial. In short, Whites and Blacks end up in unions which often perpetuate white supremacy and black self-hate, all possibly unknown to either of them at conscious levels. However, subjectively, when a Caucasian rejects white supremacy and feels estranged from "Whites" as a collective entity, almost certainly that person will seek out personal and intimate relationships among people of color. The intuitive sense tells the person within that he or she cannot spiritually survive in the violence and deadness, the corruption of the white world.

In the final analysis, then, genetic grafting in the form of intermarriage would have a positive effect from the view of one seeking to destroy white supremacy and to return all to the source of originality, on all levels: physiologically, emotionally, mentally, culturally.

My understanding of Dr. Frances Welsing's "color confrontation" thesis is that it is based on the assumption that Whites fear genetic annihilation by darker people and at the same time endure psychological stress because of the desire to be like the original. On the one hand there is a psychological impulse to destroy black, but on the other hand there is a psychological desire to be like it (thus, the sun-tanning phenomenon among Whites).[5]

Her thesis has strong support from historical evidence. White slavemasters constantly feared slave uprisings and the white males in particular would be threatened by the presence of another type of male in their social construct. White males have always exhibited psychological anxiety towards Black male sexuality. White males such as Georgia's founder, General James Edward Oglethorpe, was reported to be a "negro-phobe", greatly fearing slave uprisings. He prohibited slavery on the books, but of course it was the economic mainstay of the colony and later state. Nearly 50% of the total population of Georgia by 1850 was black.[6]

Robert Brock, a longstanding authority on and appellant for Reparations for Black slave descendants in America, points out that "for 200 years Blacks outnumbered whites 3 to 1 in North America." Indentured servants, he maintains, were brought here to offset the number of slaves.[7]

Recent demographic statistics presented by Chin Long Chiang, the leading theoretician of vital statistics, at the International Statistical Institute in Paris, reveal the number of non-Hispanic white people in the United *States* is shrinking--3.6 percent per decade. In other words, in ten years there will be 9.5 million fewer white Americans than there are now. The new projections presented by Chiang estimate that the black population is increasing about twice as fast as white numbers are declining. "If current rates were to continue, the number of blacks and non-Hispanic whites would be equal in 180 *years.* "[8](Chiang, of course, doesn't seem to take into account the ongoing genocidal assault on Black people, black men in particular, via inner city health hazards, drugs, the so- called war on drugs, inadequate housing, homelessness, incarcerations, police brutality, etc.)

Welsing's thesis is convincing, especially trying to understand "black" from the white supremacist perspective and indeed warrants Blacks and all non-white peoples, to be aware of and ready for genocidal attempts on all levels.

I would take Welsing's thesis to another level and an additional perspective: the spiritual level and a conscious level, and from the perspective of a Caucasian who would have no identification with and conscious disavowal of white supremacy. From this perspective, the reality of Blackness would not be threatening, but if anything appealing. For the truth and reality of blackness, historically and existentially, would be absorbed by consciousness rather than rejected in fear. I would maintain that both on a subconscious and conscious level, Whites in general inwardly either admire or envy not just skin color (physical appearance) as Welsing suggests, but also the presence of soul, a spiritual human quality. African descended people have consistently displayed throughout history an overwhelming presence of human power, genetic wholeness, and personal cohesion or integrity, a kind of spiritual clarity that seems to accompany the deeds of black people in all areas of life, whether it be in music, religion, athletics, science --all are imbued with a spiritual power and vision that give off an aura of certitude, precision, clarity and endurance. The pyramids and other great Nile Valley monuments attest to this, as well as the contemporary actions of Blacks today.

The problem comes when Whites collectively (in history) cover up this truth about Black people, and when they inwardly let the envy turn to hate, fueled by fear, and thus develop the counter-psychological tactic of white supremacy. This is when the White mind then attempts to both steal and destroy what Blacks have done and can do.

But if a white person does NOT see from supremacist heart and mind, then that person can only view Blackness as instructive, encompassing, original, inspirational, and ultimately personally relevant. On an intimate level, then, Blackness threatens the genitalia and generative power of white supremacists; but for the Caucasian free of the supremacist disease, Blackness is impressively real, there before anything else is, and certainly non-threatening, but more so comforting. Hence, there is the possibility of union not on the basis of domination and race denial, but on the basis of spiritual connection and personal liberation.

Most intimate relationships are hardly this dearcut and logically entered into. Such relationships are usually always unique, specific, and seldom rooted in rational debates over genetic annihilation or survival. They are simply love stories and affairs that somehow emerge out of these more opaque and complex mixtures of cultural, historical, and physiological factors.

The consideration of grafting in terms of intermarriage over a long period of time cannot be dismissed as a significant factor in the destruction of white supremacy, and the return of the Caucasian to an original nature, which is on the whole, a nature most have never known. I would hope to see further genetic research which not only establishes African (Black) origins, but which expresses and delineates the emotional, mental, and spiritual differences which accompany genetic mutation, or put another way, which accompany the presence or absence of *melanin*. This kind of biochemical research, preferably by Blacks themselves, which would illuminate the properties of melanin and how they help to form human nature and ultimately human culture would be a benefit for all people. The continuation of the annual Melanin Conferences should bring about this kind of knowledge so crucial at this time.

THE WAY OF ISLAM

If the Caucasian could not be grafted back into original nature (that is, a nature of righteousness), according to Elijah Muhammad, then he or she could attain righteousness through faith, that is, by coming into the way of Islam. Elijah Muhammad told his companions and followers that there were quite a few white believers in Islam; that he had met many of them. "They are sincere in faith," he said. He also told them there would be quite a few thousand in America, "but you will not learn of them at the present time."[9]

And he spoke of the many Caucasian Muslims in Europe, and that there were already quite a few white people in America who were Muslim by faith. As a whole race or people, however, it does not seem that Elijah Muhammad thought Whites would accept Islam, but on individual basis he acknowledged those who did.[10]

Significantly, he said of the Caucasian Muslim:

Because of their faith in Islam, Allah (God) blesses them and they will see the hereafer Good done by any person is rewarded and those white people who believe in Islam will receive the Blessing of entering into the Hereafter.[11]

What then, is the way of Islam, that it would nullify the error of white supremacy and liberate people from both enslavement and false consciousness? Simply put, it is the way of nature; the way of life that is in accord with the natural order. Ritualized, it means adhering to the practice of five basic principles: 1) Belief in One Creator, the Originator and Sustainer of the universe; 2) Prayer, 3) Fasting, 4) Charity, and 5) Pilgrimage.

These principles or pillars are the foundation of everyday life, starting with the conviction in one's heart of the reality and power of One on whom the self depends for origin and sustenance. Once this conviction is ruling within the heart, then prayer becomes the order of the day. From oeginning to end, the day is punctuated by moments of prayer to properly order one's being in the universe. The self then acquires discipline through fasting, learning to control basic appetites and to strengthen the will power to endure hardship and deprivation, and to negate any inclination to excessive habits that result in disrupting the order in the natural realm, whether it be in one's own body or in the community, which should be arranged in a manner of equity and sufficiency.

A further principle which guides one through the day and throughout life is that of charity--sharing, giving over any surplus to those more in need, and even giving of one's own share, no matter how small, to those more in need.

Lastly, while prayer takes one into the inner terrain of self, and the connection to the divine within, pilgrimage guides one outwardly towards common bonding and unity with others. While a Muslim aspires to go to Mecca for Hajj or Pilgrimage at least once in his or her life, the principle of hajj is an ongoing spirit within the person that reaches out to seek knowledge and move about the universe so that one might connect and unite with other members of the universe, thus bringing about unity and harmony.

When we look closely at these basic principles, we see that they establish a way of life which is totally opposite to the foundations of western culture and the entire corporate capitalistic white world. As established in Chapter One, the western way of life and rule is based on greed, the fueling of basic appetites, and making financial gain off these appetitive gratifications. It is a way of life also based on private personal accumulation of wealth, so that any principle of sharing and just division of resources and money is negated by the selfish desire to "get it all" and keep it, even if another goes without and suffers.

The powers maintaining modern western society do not seek to order the day with moments of prayer, but rather through media the day is filled with reminders of appetitive gratification. One is counseled to *consume* constantly, to satisfy appetites, to seek entertainment and comfort. And of utmost significance is the western axiology of ethnic and class division, color consciousness, and competition. Whereas the mentality of pilgrimage seeks to extend and connect with all members of the universe in a righteous way, the white supremacist mindset seeks to isolate, divide, heighten differences, contain, control, and conquer in order to maintain its illusion of superiority and greatness.

The way of Islam, if truly practiced by enough people in North America, would destroy the rule of white supremacy and neo-colonial capitalism, because the latter are based on principles exactly the opposite those of Islam. Islam is a way, a system of life rooted in generosity, generation, nurturance. An exploitive system like capitalistic North America, however, feeds on weakened victims and sucks their labor and life from them. Islamic systems thrive on mutual giving and maintaining of members.

This is why Malcolm X said his by now oft-quoted words regarding Whites and Islam after his return from Mecca. Here is some of what he said :

America needs to understand Islam, because this is the one religion that erases from its society the race problem. Throughout my travels in the Muslim world, I have met, and talked to, and even eaten with people who in American would have been considered "white" —but the "white' attitude was removed from their minds by the religion of Islam. I have never before seen sincere and true brotherhood practiced by all colors together, irrespective of their color We were truly all the same (brothers) —because their belief in one God has removed the "white" from their minds, the "white" from their behavior, and the "white" from their atti tude.

I could see from this that perhaps if white Americans could accept the Oneness of God, then perhaps, too, they could accept in reality the Oneness of Man --cease to measure, and hinder, and harm others in terms of their "difference" in color.[12]

In essence, Malcolm X was only reiterating what his teacher and spiritual father, Elijah Muhammad, had taught him: that Islam could liberate not only the lost- found Nation of Blacks in the Wilderness of North America by giving them knowledge of the One Creator and themselves, but also those Whites who genuinely sought to establish truth for themselves and oppose the forces of oppression that characterized the white western form of rule.

It is significant how much media commentary followed Malcolm X's statement, and yet how very few Whites seemed to take seriously the counsel he had extended. Instead, most interpreted his words as "vindicating" Whites from all that Elijah Muhammad had taught about them. They therefore failed to explore in any meaningful way why white people in Mecca seemed different to him, nor did it lead them to question in any deep way the psychological malaise of white supremacy.

When considering the five principles discussed above, we understand that Elijah Muhammad was demonstrating unity and commonality with Muslims allover the world. But beyond that, Islam, for Elijah Muhammad, seemed to mean much more in America. It had a mission of its own and one that only could be fulfilled here, on the shores of the wilderness of North America. Elijah Muhammad stated that the principles remain the same always, but he indicated a number of times that Islam in America would move, change and bring about an entirely new order of things.

Islam in America by definition had to deal with color. It was the only way for the oppressed Black population to extricate itself from white domination and rule; from the graveyard of the Bible and white Christianity. Islam was the way out of conditions of hell in which white people had placed African slaves and their descendants. Islam was the knowledge which was waking up and illuminating the dead negro (Lazarus) to his original nature, his self worth, and destiny in life. It was a methodology of knowing self by knowing the past of both ancestors and the ancestors' oppressors. It was a religion, a way of life, that instructed its adherents to seek out knowledge and understanding. It did not counsel them to seek highly charged emotional staies and moments of mystic vision. Instead, it counseled them to seek the knowledge that would unlock the chains on their minds and would illuminate the conditions of life in which they had been floundering. Elijah Muhammad masterfully unfolded both the Bible and Holy Qur'an to demonstrate and instruct his people on what had been done to them, and what needed to be done by them in order to arrive at freedom, justice, and equality.

Consequently, the media soon identified Islam, in North America at least, as a black thing. The members of the Nation of Islam were called Black Muslims, and in time, were called nothing but this in major media. And Black Muslims were characterized as violent, racist, and potentially disruptive to the American way of life.

White people in this country had never really been exposed to Islam as a religion or way of life. Those who were involved in freemasonry had some knowledge of Islam, but the code of secrecy in masonry forbade them to share it openly. The coverups discussed in Chapter One were essential to keeping not only Blacks ignorant of true history and self knowledge, but also to keep the majority of white Americans unaware of the realities of origins and the truth of themselves. White western Christianity served to lock both Blacks and Whites into false consciousness. Its caucasoid imagery, including a white god that would adorn the walls of churches and homes across the country, across the world, locked African slave descendants into psychological traps of self-denial, self-hatred and hellish conditions of life that seemed to accompany the mere fact of being Black. The same imagery and imposter god locked Caucasians into a mindset of supremacy and self- aggrandizement. Western Christianity perpetrated fraud on all, and Elijah Muhammad's Islamic mission was to uncover and expose this massive set of lies and grand theft. This exposure of worldwide racism and religious fraud could only come from the depths, the bottom of the social structure that had taken shape because of these events.

Old World Muslims could not deliver this kind of Islam, for they had not lived in the belly of the beast (America), nor had they been enslaved (although the African Bilal, the first prayer caller, *muezzin,* whom Prophet Muhammad chose to institute that important ritual had been a slave). Also, not just a few Old World Muslims had fallen victim themselves to the westernization of the mind and habits of life. They could not come to the U.S. and expect to "convert" people in this country to Islam as a religion and NOT deal with the issue of color and the crimes of the white race as a whole. But many did come in this manner, extending the Qur'an and knowledge of Arabic, the five principles, articles of faith, the life of the Prophet, but usually without ever identifying the evil embodied in the white supremacist government or its racist religion, not to mention its political and economic strategies of colonialism and capitalism. Some came to the United States and attained more education, lucrative employment, and financial security. They could go to mosque on Friday for jumah prayer, make salat (prayer) at home, fast during Ramadhan, all without pointing a finger at the American government, its system, and its heinous history. They were perhaps unawares in complicity with this oppressive system. Some privatized their religion like most Americans, taking on the routine of work and private accumulation of wealth. Communal prayer on Friday became almost like church on Sunday for the Christians. Because of the privacy of career and work, the five prayers got pushed to the end of the day to be "made Up."

Elijah Muhammad wisely and with determination never failed to see Islam as a way to disentangle oneself from white America, to separate from its religious lies and cover-ups, and its malicious economic system of exploitation. The true Muslim therefore would stand out firmly against white racism and oppose those who perpetuated it. There could be no *"safe* keeping" in the belly of the beast (white America), nor negotiations with its representatives. Indeed, America was the ground for Islamic Jihad, a total struggle on all fronts, using all faculties, against mental and physical oppression, and a commitment to full and complete liberation. From this perspective, Islam was revolutionary, hardly accomodationist.

THE NEW ISLAM

Elijah Muhammad very clearly in *Message* to *the Blackman in America,* states that a new Islam will emerge in America, and he further says that Old World Muslims will oppose it. The Orthodox Muslims will have to bow to the choice of Allah. Allah will bring about a new Islam. As for the Principles of Belief, they remain the same. There will be no more signs to be watched for the coming of God and the setting up of a new world of Islam. We are seeing this change now and entering into it. The devils oppose this change, and the Orthodox join them in opposing us because of their desire to car-ryon the old way of Islam.[13]

He also used the Bible to get this message across, stating: There are many Muslims who do not care to read anything in the Bible. But those Muslims have not been given my job The coming of a "New World," or a new order of things, is very hard for the people of the Old World to believe. Therefore, they are opposed to the New World.[14]

He also spoke of a "Last Book:"

There is another Book that none has been able to see or read, its contents coming soon from Allah--the "Last Book," which takes us i nto the hereafter.[15]

A distinct aspect of Islam as Elijah Muhammad articulated it was its connection to Black originality, long before Judaism, Christianity, and Islam became identified in western terminology as the major "Great Religions." Elijah Muhammad made the African connection, that is, the connection of Islam to its most ancient form and root.

By expressing this understanding, he rescued Islam from the shallow thinking that has placed it as a new religion "founded" by Prophet Muhammad, and built upon Judaism and Christianity. (It is the other way around, Judaism and Christianity were built on Islam before it was called Islam.) These later religions built upon and took from the ancient way as it was expressed in old Kemet (ancient Egypt), the Nile Valley before the Pyramids even. Says Elijah Muhammad :

Many of you sing that old song, "Give Me That Old Time Religion." Islam is that "old time religion." It is as old as God himself, and God is the author of Islam. Islam was not invented as is the case of Christianity and other religions. Islam came with Allah (God) and the universe.[16]

Islam understood in this manner firmly locates it as the way of god (Allah)--the way embedded in nature itself and the original nature of people. Therefore, out of the darkness of the beginning and original peoples came the light of Islam, as a way of being and living in the world. This bared and simple understanding of Islam paves the way for it to accomplish the mission of eliminating the world of racist, nationalistic supremacy, and the use of that perpetrated and fraudulent power to generate systems of life which exploit and drain people of their humanity, such as the system of white American corporate capitalism.

The new Islam will usher in an era of justice, the hereafter following the demise of the western white system of rule. This moment of islamitization of the planet does not mean individual people the world over will throw themselves to the ground in the familiar form of Muslim prayer, or stampede the mosques, or even call themselves Muslim. Rather, it will be a time of returning things to balance. It will admtnister justice, because justice is precisely the establishment of balance. Min. Farrakhan, the National Representative of Elijah Muhammad and the Nation of Islam has said that Elijah Muhammad spoke of the best religion as being the religion ofjustice.[17]

This reaching back and returning the planet to its original order can only come through the knowledge and wisdom of those whose roots extend back beyond European rule and the establishment of western religion. African slave descendants and Native indigenous peoples of the Americas hold the wisdom to restore order, balance, and harmony. They also, being the most oppressed and despised, are the ones best equipped and motivated to destroy white rule and the unjust social systems accompanying that rule.

AMERICA, THE SOIL OF A NEW ISLAM

The land mass called America (the Americas, North and South), and specifically the United States, contains the presence of these two ancient peoples whose roots extend into the originality of Islam, or the natural way. It is not by chance that Hopi means peace, as does Islam and Muslim. This peace comes about through total submission to the natural order as designed in the Originator's Thought. It is not by chance that to see through Hopi eyes is to see things in balance, as is the way of seeing from Muslim vision. Nor is it an accident that the Hopi constitute the oldest presence of the indigenous people on this soil, descended from the " Ancient Ones," the Anasazi. These "signs" let us know there is a oneness among the peoples and in their ways of life. The African presence on this soil has roots extending into the source of life itself, the ancient soil of generation before its recording. Africa and America were wedded together long before the Europeans came, and before history was recorded.

The convergence of these two peoples on this soil provides the fertile seed ground for generating a new way out of the old way which will be free of the white man's rule and the evils we combat today under the labels of racism, sexism, imperialism or neo-colonialism. This is why, I believe, Elijah Muhammad predicted that Old World Muslims would oppose the new Islam; because so much of the old Muslim world has, in time, found a way to psychologically claim to be Muslim and live according to the rituals and habits of Islamic life, while at the same time doing this in the context of a western culture or climate of exploitation. Saudi Arabia is the most visible sign of this dualism, this profession of Islam and at the same time broad and far-reaching collaboration with western political and economic forces. (An exception would be Muslims who are represented in the attitude of the publication " *New Trend,*" an independent forum for the oppressed Muslim masses, published in this country).[18]

This is why the American soil has to generate its own form of Islam (on the same basic five principles) but with a revolutionary spirit and justice-seeking. Only Muammar AI Qathafi of the Islamic world has come forth to speak explicitly on the color issue (which is *the* issue shrouding all the ills of social inequity today}. In his *Green Book,* Qathafi devotes an entire chapter to "The Blacks." He says:

The latest age of slavery is the white race's enslavement of the black race. The black man will not forget this until he has achieved rehabilitation.[19]

Qathafi goes on to say "Now comes the Black race's turn to prevail." And he also sees the way of contemporary times, the way of Islam, as the way of the masses, the rule of the people. The revolutionary movement and democracy that Libya has instituted is called the *Jamahiriyat,* that is, the authority of the people. It is not unusual at all that he has extended firm and moral support to the Nation of

Islam under Min. Farrakhan, who is continuing the work of Elijah Muhammad at this time. Qathafi also has hosted an International Conference for the Liberation of Indian Peoples of the Americas (held in Tripoli, January-February, 1988). Some 150 representa- tives of 25 indigenous nations, tribes and organizations from 15 countries in the western hemisphere and the Pacific met to mobilize a stronger liberation thrust to a united Indian Front, looking beyond tribal distinction to a universal order or peace and mutual harmony once the evils of white rule have been eliminated.[20]

Is it any wonder that the United States Government has exerted such tremendous intelligence and military effort to both discredit and eliminate Muammar Qathafi? The disinformation tactics a few years back portrayed him as a mad man, a neurotic, and even a sexual deviant, making references to his clothes, personal habits and psychological state. It was revealed publicly of course afterwards that this was a deliberate disinformation campaign to discredit Qathafi.

President Reagan went further on to order the bombing of the Bab Al-Aziziyah barracks which served as Qathafi's home, on April 15, 1986. His 15-month old adopted daughter was killed, two other children of Qathafi were injured, and his wife hospitalized. The U.S. Air Force were responsible for releasing the bombloads that dealt this murder. How appropriate that the first anniversary of this tragic event was commemorated by close to 500 people at the site, where an American Indian youth climbed a 15 feet high torch and lit it.[21]

White Americans on the whole seemed to miss the real meaning of this entire propagandistic and militaristic demonstration on the part of the U.S. Government, and in Public Enemy's words, they believed "the hype." But the message here is a repeat of Public Enemy's: "don't believe the hype! " Likewise, Americans have so easily believed that Muslims are violent; that Arabs are violent; that mid- easterners on the whole are "terrorists." They have believed the hype and they identify Islam as a violent religion. Americans, white Americans in particularl are greatly confused about who is who; who is violentl who is a terrorist.

In contrast, I recall seeing posters in Northwest Washington, D.C., not long after the bombing, all along the streets, on light posts, corner signs, walls of buildings, whose words expressed solidarity with Qathafi and clearly identified the U.S. Government as a murderer and bomber of babies. This revealed to me how aware the inner city Black population is and how out of touch with international as well as domestic reality most white Americans are. I am not sure who put the signs up, possibly not black people at all; but the point is, they stayed up in black D.C. They would not have been popular in suburbia nor allowed to remain publicly visible.

Islam in America (and not the" American Islam" that the deceased Ayatollah Khomeini used to condemn as the Old World accomodationist brand of lslam)l as a truly new and inspired Islam has the distinct and unique ability to eliminate divisions, fragmentations, and inequities, while binding people together in a simple return to the basics of the natural order and human community. What I mean by this is that the insidious and intense effects of white racism and its capitalistic economics has caused people who once identified themselves solely by tribal distinctions, to look beyond differences in order to unite on a common basis of oppression in an effort to achieve liberation. For examplel a basic theme of Sterling stuckey's excellent book on *Slave Culture* is that of demonstrating how African tribal differences soon faded in the onslaught of brutal slavery in this country and Blacks began to identify more on the basis of their common condition. A "slave culture" even developed which included critical strategies for survival and self defense.[22]

So too have Native Americans done this. The International conference mentioned above is only one example. Native peoples have since the 60's especially demonstrated that tribal and sovereign distinctions need not be forfeited in a united effort to stand up against the oppressions and devastating effects of white rule in their native lands. The 1969 occupation of Alcatraz Island was conducted by a group called Indians of All Tribes. The 1972 "Trail of Broken Treaties" caravan made up of Indians from allover the country descended on Washington, D.C.

It is the presence of these descendants of ancients in the entrails of the New World, the United States, that provides a threshold to new life and restored balance. Because both peoples have vision and traditions, that predate the shaping of the New World, predate European so-called civilization, they can retrieve that wisdom, that methodology whereby people can live a truly human life.

It is significant that any time an oppressed people such as

Blacks and Native Americans begin to unite among themselves and then with each other in demonstrations of resistance towards continued domestic colonization, their calls for separation from white America and self- determination are met with extreme hostility by the Government. The general public follows along, bolstered by media, in viewing them as "racist separatists," who oppose the principles of "democracy" and egalitarianism. Of course the same public will cheer on an ethnic population or a Republic of the Soviet Union when it rises up in demonstrations for independence. What it amounts to is that the U.S. Government and the ruling elite would just as soon get rid of both Blacks and Native Americans. Black labor is no longer for free nor even for cheap hire; Blacks in America want justice and reparations, no more leftovers. Native Americans now know how to go about legally reclaiming their stolen lands and regain sovereignty.

But the bulk of American white middle class people don't want to let go. They don't want to see such "separation" because it means the system isn't what it's cracked up to be afterall. They want to hear "I Have a Dream" speech over and over, while sitting in some candle-lit public event or holding hands in a school or community gathering, believing in the American Dream; they want it to be true, not understanding that for it to be true they would have to lose half or more of what they possessed.

Simply put, the real separatist has always been the white separatist who, as a tiny minority of the world's population, has tried to rule the world in a way that maximizes their own profits and benefits of life while keeping the majority of world's population separated from each other and suffering in intolerable and immensely oppressive living conditions. To separate from the white separatist and supremacist is to join in the *human* family which seeks freedom, justice and equality. To separate from white America is to become human.

When I try to get this last point across to students in my college and university classes, I am often confronted with a total silence, and a room of faces which display emotions of doubt, trouble, fear, and confusion. Inevitably, someone will ask: "But what other way is there?" A kind of hopelessness and impending danger prevails in the room. The very thought has already tugged at the foundations of their world. Throughout the class for approximately four months, they have shown disbelief and sometimes anger that the U.S. Government and corporate America could carry out such oppressive operations as the relocation and genocide of native peoples; the enslavement and genocide of African descended people; the nuclear terrorism of military build- up and hazardous nuclear sites with lethal waste; the neglect and disavowal of the homeless; and the aggressive terroristic military invasions of Third World countries, not to mention germ and biological experimentation and warfare. As the evidence piles up and the system gets more scrutinized, those who have dared to question that far feel abandoned in a world falling apart, sometimes they feel betrayed; but most never get that far. Most reject the evidence, block it out; most refuse to seriously ask the questions. Most would never consider leaving America in their minds. They cling to the illusionary dream, while failing to see the real world, the planet Earth, dying in their arms, beneath their feet, all around.

For those who have gone further to question and depart from the white western cui de sac, there is this new spirit, this falling into the embrace of the universe, which opens the way for "salvation." Call it the new Islam, or simply the way of righteousness, it is a way made possible at this time by the enduring, uncompromising swell of original peoples as they struggle towards liberation, pulling forth from the depths of darkness all that is necessary to clarify, justify and avenge, as well as establish in truth a new order of things. For the white person who has departed from White America in mind and heart, he or she must now follow in the path of the ancients and bend to the earth in submission, realizing that it is this Mother that gave us life and the laws governing it. It is this return to the Origination that brings about salvation.

SAVING MOTHER EARTH AND THE RETURN OF THE MATERNAL

The salvation of white men and women lies in heeding the wisdom and behavioral directives that are now being articulated by African and Native indigenous peoples, the inheritors of the Secrets, that were stolen and further concealed by white invaders who penetrated both Africa and the so-called New World. *Human* salvation lies in saving the planet Earth.

It is interesting that when one consults the dictionary about the word *human,* one is led to the root Latin word *homo,* meaning man, and not to the word *humus,* which means earth. But after leading you to *homo,* the definition says "more at homage." So when one turns to *homage,* one is finally led to *humus,* and then is told : "more at humble." Homage of course is not the same as humble; it relates to man elevating a man over him; flattering a man, like a vassal deferring to his lord (not *the* Lord). But when one turns to *humble,* he or she finds the true nature of man: "not proud or haughty," nor " arrogant. " It is a postu re of *submission.* It took a long way through Websterian detours to find oneself identified, but ultimately, one is taken back to earth. Understanding the laws embedded in Mother Earth is the key to human nature.[23]

The way of Islam is the way of submission to the natural order. It calls for establishing one's personal life in harmony with the natural processes of life which operate on principles of cooperation, mutual aid, economy or sufficiency, not an economy of accumulation. The ancient wisdom of original peoples counsels one to study the laws of nature which constitute the universe without and the universe within. When these laws are known and respected, peace and order reign, both throughout the universe and within the self.

In submitting to the ways of the natural order, one becomes a member of that order, not its lord, not its subduer, never its aggressor and violator. Such a person is at *home* in the universe, governed by its laws. The self is one with the universe; no fears of extinction, nor even of inadequacy because one is empowered by the spirit of human capacity and the universal energy connecting us all together .

To arrive at this attitude of respect towards the primacy and power of Mother Earth, one is in fact humbly deferring to the feminine principle and maternal power throughout the universe and within oneself, whether one is man or woman. The human community must establish once again the *presence* of the feminine principle in everyday life; the maternal power must be re-instated so that balance can be restored.

The feminine maternal principle brings continuance, stability and endurance to life. It guards the sacred properties of life itself. When it is present, the earth and its members are not to be subjected

135

to abuse in the form of rape, desecration, violation, and murder. One understands these terms when applied to woman; but how does one rape the earth? Mining. Strip-mining and all other mining penetrates the sacred cavities of the earth; she is robbed of her wealth; she is left barren and empty. How does one violate, desecrate the earth? So many ways. Dumping toxic waste; spraying pesticides; releasing chemicals and germs into the atmosphere. And murder? Study the rain-forests. Look at the death.

It was the European who engaged in these violations. Indigenous people the world over lived in harmony with the Earth; and therefore, they lived in harmony amongst themselves. The maternal spirit governed their relations. It was the white male who sought to eliminate the maternal, the feminine. The western world is patriarchal, male dominated. It has left a trail of history full of aggression, violation and destruction. When the masculine principle is left to run rampant and rule, death and destruction seem to overwhelm life and generation.

Paula Gunn Allen, speaking from the Native indigenous view, expresses it th is way:

The male principle is transitory; it dies and is reconstituted. The female principle, which is immanent in hard substances (like the earth, minerals, crystals, and stones), wood, and water, is permanent; it remains. Male is breath, air, wind, and projectile point; female controls, creates, and u owns" breath, air and wind, bird and feather, and the hard substance from which the projectile point is shaped. Female is earth, sun, moon, sky, water in its multitudinous forms and its evergenerating cycle, corn, mother of the deer, mother of the gods, bringer of fire and light, and fire itself (which is why the women are its keepers among many if not most groups). He is what comes and goes, she is what continues and stays.[24]

A people will die without the power of the feminine, the enduring maternal. Paula Allen speaks of this principle in traditional Native images: WISDOM

Do the #1

...She is the Old Woman who tends the fires of life. She is the Old Woman Spider who weaves us together in a fabric of interconnections. She is the Eldest God, the one who Remembers and Re-members; and

136

*though the history of the past five hundred years has taught us bitterness
and helpless rage, we endure into the present, alive, certain of our significance, certain of her centrality, her identity as the Sacred Hoop of
Being.*[25]

In the spirit of being in harmony with this universal movement of the restoration of balance, Min. Farrakhan of the Nation of
Islam has often emphasized the primacy and power of the woman. He
recently renamed and dedicated the newly renovated mosque and
educational center in Chicago as "Mosque Maryam," an appropriate
new beginning for the re-education of his people, Black people, and
ultimately the re-establishment of the natural order throughout the
universe.

Elijah Muhammad often taught his people that the life or
demise of a nation could be gauged by the condition and status of its
women. Similarly, Paula Allen brings to our attention the old
Cheyenne wisdom, "no people is broken until the heart of its women
is on the ground."[26]

The way of salvation is the way of bringing together the masculine and feminine principles so that balance prevails and justice is
done. At this cosmic and universal level, the small-minded and fearful ideologies of color supremacy and economics of greed, are blatantly insufficient for personal satisfaction and planetary survival.

White supremacy is destroyed by becoming human; becoming a member of the universe; a part of the Medicine Wheel, a seg-
ment of the Sacred Hoop; a point on the circle of life, which empow-
ers us to come and go as the Creator so designed us to do, manifest-
ing His/Her All-Power.

NOTES

(Chapter Four)

1.)   Elijah Muhammad, *Our Saviour Has Arrived* (Chicago: Muhammad's Temple of Islam, No.2, 1974), p. 200.

2.)   *Ibid.*, pp. 77-78.

3.)   Mamie Garvin Fields, with Karen Fields, *Lemon Swamp and Other Places: A Carolina Memoir* (N. y .: The Free Press, 1983), Chapters 12 and 13.

4.)   Reprint of" Another Call from the Hopi," 1977, in *Akwesasne Notes* (Publication of the Mohawk Nation) Winter, 1989.

5.)   See Frances Cress Welsing, *Cress Theory of Color Confrontation* (Washington, D.C.: C-R Publications, 1970). Also interview .series with Welsing by listervelt Middleton aired on "For the People," South Carolina Educational Television, in 1990).

6.)   "Savannah's Amazing Grace," in *American Heritage* (February,1989).

7.)   Quoted in *The National Newport News & Commentator* (January/February 1990). Also see other reparations materials distributed by the Self Determination committee, 8223 South Broadway, L.A., Calif., 90003.

8.)   "Demography: The Shifting U.S. Racial Mix," in the *Washington Post* (January 1, 1990).

9.)   Elijah Muhammad, *Our Saviour Has Arrived, op. cit.,* p. 83.

10.) See Elijah Muhammad, *The Supreme Wisdom: Solution to the Socal'ed Negroes' Problem* (Newport News, Va.: The National Newport News and Commentator, fi rst edition, 1957), p. 30.

11.) *Our Saviour Has Arrived, op. cit.,* p. 89.

12.) Malcolm X, *The Autobiography of Malcolm X*, with the assist ance of Alex Haley (N. y .: Grove Press, 1964), pp. 340-341.

13.) *Message to the Blackman, op. cit:.* pp. 49-50.

14.) *Ibid.*, pp. 82-83.

15.) *Ibid.,p.91.*

16.) *Ibid.*, pp. 79-80.

17.) Audio Cassette, Min. Farrakhan Speaks, "The Day of

Vengeance: Allah the Killer," September 10, 1989.

18.) See *New Trend,* published by the American Society for Education & Religion, Inc., P.O. Box 356, Kingsville, Md. 21087.

19.) Muammar AI Qathafi, *The Green Book,* p. 45 (no further publication information).

20.) See *Pan-African Roots* (Chicago: The Independent and Progressive Voice of African People Around the World, Volume 1, No.1, March 1-17, 1988.

21.) See *Final Call* (May 15, 1987).

22.) Sterling Stuckey, *Slave Culture: Nationalist Theory and the Foundations of Black America* (Oxford University Press, 1988).

23.) *Webster's New Collegiate Dictionary* (Springfield, Mass.: G. and C. Merriam Co., 1974).

24.) Paula Gunn Allen, *The Sacred Hoop: Recovering the Feminine in American Indian Traditional* (Boston: Beacon Press, 1986), p. 267.

25.) *Ibid.,p.11.*

26.) *Ibid.,* p. 267.

EPILOGUE

THE BOTTOM LINE

The bottom line is Black. Any person who wants to clarify and arrive at the entire picture of how the world got to be in the condition it is today must take the journey back to origins, to all the truth of life and civilization before Europe ever was and before white America. And then one needs to come all the way through the shades of humanity to where we are now.

This means that white people who truly desire this clarification must become students of history, and history as it is now being corrected and accurately written by scholars (from the streets as well as the university) who are uncovering and exposing the hidden parts that were concealed and distorted by white supremacist historians through the years.

To perform this kind of intensive recostruction of history and one's own world-view, Caucasians must be in touch with the Black Liberation Movement in all of its manifestations, as well as the Movements among Native American peoples to attain liberation, sovereignty and an authentic history written from their own experience and perspective. For it is within the various segments of these movements that the historical and scientific research is being brought to light.

The question inevitably arises: how does the white person stay in touch with these non-white movements? Should one join some organiztaion? I always recall Malcolm X's words on this matter.

...I have these very deep feelings that white people who want to join black organizations are really just taking the escapist way to salve their consciences. By visibly hovering near us, they are "proving" they are "with us." But the hard truth is this isn't helping to solve America's racist problem. The negroes aren't the racists. Where the really sincere white people have got to do their "proving" of themselves is not among the black victims, but out on the battle lines of where America's racism

really is—and that's in their own home communities; America's racism is among their own fellow whites, that's where the sincere whites who really mean to accomplish something have got to work.[1]

Malcolm said this around 1965, near the end of his life. No one can really say how Malcolm X might answer the question today, but I suspect it would be very near the same thing. He did, at the same time the above was spoken, go on to say:

I tell sincere white people, "Work in conjuction with us—each of us working among our own king. "...

and,

We will completely respect our white co-wokers. They will deserve every credit. We will give them every credit. We will meanwhile be working among our own kind, in our own black communities—showing and teaching black men in ways that only black men can—that the black man has got to help himself. Working separately, the sincere white people and sincere Black people actually will be working together.[2]

Malcolm concluded that "in our mutual sincerity we might be able to show a road to the salvation of America's very soul."

What Malcolm X didn't mention was the ver essential need for the sincere Whites to be in constant touch with the knowledge, history and direction coming forth from the Black Liberation Movement. My own life experience let me understand that any Caucasian who wants to find out the real truth must in some way be in touch with what's being said and unfolded by Blacks, Native Americans, any non-white people who are struggling to liberate both lives and knowledge. In the late 60's and early 70's, I found myself being drawn to the movements of Black people. Despite my pocket full of degrees (and I might add "miseducation"), I found myself looking towards the streets, the campuses, and inner cities, anywhere I heard Blacks articulating both the past and the present. I didn't particulartly seek to join anything, but I wanted to be close to the truth I felt was coming forth from these efforts, and attended whatever public events I could to gain understanding.

When I consciously identified as Muslim, I wanted to be a

part of the Nation of Islam, as my husband had, but its membership was restricted to Blacks at the time, (1971). While living in Canada I did consult with Orthodox Muslims at a local mosque, but their disavowal of the Honorable Elijah Muhammad, and signs of westernization dettered me from continuing any participation. I was hungry for the truth,and gathered all I could from the Islamic instructions of my husband and the weekly radio broadcasts of the Nation of Islam's National Spokesman at the time, Min. Louis Farrakhan. While I did want to learn about making prayers in Arabic, reading the Qur'an, knowing the history of Prophet Muhammad (P.b.u.h.), I was driven to know the truth of the past I had been a part of--I needed to understand white America. It seemed I could find both in the teaching of Elijah Muhammad. I could now understand the scriptures, both Bible and Qur'an, in an entirely new way, not in the old interpretations that seemed to end in mental dead end streets. Whenver I could get a hold of Muhammad Speaks Newspaper I felt an imense opening up of both past and present. I also had felt this new energy and vision when the Black Panthers articulated reality in their public lectures and newspaper.[3]

In 1975, I was permitted to join the Nation of Islam under the leadership of Imam Warith Deen Muhammad, who opened the doors to whites and all ethnic groups. Imam Muhammad was of course trying to bring the Nation more into the mainstream of Orthodox Islam. My experience and work with the brothers and sisters in Chicago and other cities was invaluable. I grew spiritually in being a part of the community as well as intellectually in gaining the knowledge necessary for understanding white America. However, when the Nation of Islam was later transformed to the American Muslim Mission, its direction seemed to be more ameliorative towards the United States. The American flag appeared in the mosque and on the paper (which had undergone various name changes). I grew uncomfortable in an atmosphere I considered to be more collaborative than revolutionary, and withdrew from active participaton.

By 1985, I had become aware of Min. Farrakhan's efforts to rebuild the Nation of Islam and complete the work of Elijah Muhammad. White I, like most Muslims and like most Blacks whether Muslim or not, really wanted to see unity rather than divisions in this struggle, I genuinely felt Min. Farrkhan's efforts were in the right direction. For a time I considered an appeal to participate in this effort as part of the Nation. But I believe I understood more clearly what Malcolm X had meant at this time than I did before. I had always felt I could be more effective as a teacher, out in the larger society rather than in a more close community though it may be one with like-minded individuals. At the same time, I felt a need to be close to the Minister's teaching and supportive of his effort. But I did not feel the Nation of Islam needed me as an active sincerity in a Caucasian, there still was a prevailing sentiment that this mission had to be completed free of white participation.

In short, Whites cannot really "help" Blacks execute their mission of total, complete liberation, except by struggling to eliminate those barriers in the larger society which have placed Blacks (and other non-European peoples) in such oppressed conditions in the first place. These barriers resulting from the rule of white supremacy (capitalism, racism, sexism) must be destroyed. The relationship between black and white in this crucial time is one of dissemination of knowledge and strategic guidance in the struggle for liberation.

One of the most appropriate groups for white people to associate with in this effort to complete the liberation struggle is the African People's Solidarity Committee. This is an organized movement of North Americans (Whites) who support the African People's Socialist Party in the liberation struggle. The Solidarity movement is about as close as anything to the format Malcolm X described as appropriate for Blacks and Whites working towards the same goal. The Solidarity Committee does not seek to cousel or guide or control the Black Liberation Movement. Rather, it works in consultation with the African People's Socialist Party in bringing about the destruction of these barriers mentioned above. It receives the instruction and strategy from APSP, and does not seek to work outside this mutual cooperation. It is part of the People's Democratic Uhuru Movement.

The rule of white supremacy has been one in which scholars and educators, writers and historians have covered up the essential truth. But Black historians, educators, writers, researchers in general have never been anything but open and generous with their knowledge. Today with the new inpiration of young and old Black scholars mutually working to bring forth the wealth of information that can correct a distorted history, there is an abundant amount of knowledge in the form of tapes, videos, books, newspapers, etc. The same is happening within the Native American Population. The many diverse groups and organizations should not deter one from seeking out the knowledge which flows from the all. White media and ruling forces committed to halting this surge of liberating knowledge coming forth from non-white sources, will seek to plant confusion and doubt in the minds of the public, by portraying the diverse groups as a warring with one another. But the wise student of history learns to see that opposites are really one; negative and positive are but different manifestations of one energy.

Today I look across the horizon of human struggle and understand that , as a Muslim, the universe is the mosque. Nature is the Book. And I can see the energy of truth and liberation pouring forth from all four corners of the universe. Some emanations of truth will be more profound than others. Some will be more "on time" than others . But all somehow converge in the unity of knowledge and the ultimate clarification of the specific moment of time we are now confronted with.

White has never been the original. It could never be without black being first. Therefore, on every level white depends on black to lead the way, and illuminate the horizion. Thus it is that out of darkness comes light.

In very practical terms, any Caucasian who wishes to be informed truthfully and to eventually contribute to the destruction of white supremacy and the oppressions of its 6,000 years of unjust rule, he or she can get a good start with the minimal suggestions for freeing the mind listed below.

SOME ESSENTIAL BOOKS TO READ

Message to the Blackman in America, by Elijah Muhammad
Our Saviour Has Arrived, by Elijah Muhammad
The Autobiography of Malcolm X, with Alex Haley
The Destruction of Black Civilization, by Chancellor Williams
African Origins of Civilization, by Cheikh Anta Diop
Ethiopia and the Origin of Civilization, by John G. Jackson
Black Man of the Nile, by Yosef ben-Jochannan

From the Browder File, by Anthony T. Browder
Agents of Repression: The FBI'S Secret War Against the Black Panther Party and the American Indian Movement, by Ward Churchill and Jim Vander Wall
How Capitalism Underdeveloped Black America, by Manning Marable
Stolen Legacy, by George G. M. James
The Sacred Hoop, by Paula Gunn Allen
The Legacy of the Hon. Elijah Muhammad, by H.K. Khalifah
Seven Speeches, by Minister Louis Farrakhan
How Europe Underdeveloped Africa, by Walter Rodney
Bread, Peace and Black Power, by Omali Yeshitela
The Iceman Inheritance, by Michael Bradley
The Hidden Wound, by Wendell Berry
Lame Deer: Seeker of Visions, by John (Fire) Lame Deer
The Came Before Columbus, by Ivan Van Sertima
Indian Givers, by Jack Weatherford
Nile Valley Civilizations, ed. by Ivan Van Sertiman

NEWSPAPERS

The Final Call (FCN Pub. Co., 734 W. 79th St., Chicago, IL, 60620)
The National Newport News & Commentator (P.O. Box 5368, Newport News, VA 23605)
Burning Spear (P.O. Box 27205, Oakland, CA 94602)
The Wire (P.O. Box 73861, T-Street Station, Washington, DC 20056)
By Any Means Necessary (P.O. Box 31762, Jackson, MO 39286)
Muslim Journal (7801 S. Cottage Grove Ave., Chicago, IL 60629)
New Trend (P.O. Box 356, Kingsville, MD 21087)
Akwesasne Notes (Mohawk Nation via Rooseveltown, NY 13683)

There are many pamphlets and books listed in these papers, as well as order information and names of bookstores all across the country.

Also listed and available are audio cassettes and video tapes of various spokespeople such as Min. Louis Farrkhan of the Nation of Islam, Chairman Omali Yeshitela of the African People's Socialist

Party, and others.

It is also suggested that one read the *Bible* and *Holy Qur 'an* from a perspective free of white Christian interpretation and imagery.

Other significant videos are: the speeches and life of Malcolm X (*El Hajj Malik El Shbazz*); History of Black Panter Party.

"Broken Rainbow" which concerns the Governmental and corporate war against Hopi and Navajo people.

The slide series on video of Dr. Asa Hillard demonstrating the African origins of humanity and evidence of its cover-up. Consult this and *Free the Mind Bibliography* (Dr. Asa Hillard, Education Foundations, Georgia State University, University Plaza, Atlanta, GA 30303)

Very significant are the *For the People* series produced by South Carolina Educational T.V., aired on local Public Broadcast Stations.

Check local black radio and t.v. in your area. Examples would be the Pacifica Foundation stations; such as WPFW in Washington D.C. (Pacifica is not solely a "black" network, nor black owned, but includes a very reliable Afro-centrinc formant).

NOTES

(Epilogue)

1.)   *The Autobiography of Malcolm X,* with the assistance of Alex Haley (N.Y. :Grove Press, 1966 edition), p. 376

2.)   *Ibid.,* p. 377

3.)   A more autobiographical and detailed account of these expe riences are included in the unpublished manuscript, *The Higher Self.*